Patricia Roc

Patricia Roc
the goddess of the Odeons

MICHAEL HODGSON

authorHOUSE®

AuthorHouse™ UK Ltd.
1663 Liberty Drive
Bloomington, IN 47403 USA
www.authorhouse.co.uk
Phone: 0800.197.4150

Front cover picture courtesy of ITV Studios Global international
Back cover picture courtesy of Michael Thomas

Published by AuthorHouse   08/30/2013

ISBN: 978-1-4817-6940-2 (sc)
ISBN: 978-1-4817-6941-9 (e)

For Sue, again and always

Contents

Preface and Acknowledgements

SINCE publishing *Patricia Roc – the goddess of the Odeons* in 2010 a lot of important information has come my way, including the Patricia Roc files secreted away in the J. Arthur Rank archives. Also, after reading the book, people who knew Patricia Roc have contacted me, and have added to my knowledge of the lady. It therefore seemed appropriate to revise and re-examine the first book with all this new information. The result is this much enlarged and improved edition. Also added to this edition are many more photographs, some published for the first time, and an interesting selection from Pat's treasured autograph book that she meticulously kept throughout her acting career.

So, this is not the 'old' book, but a much-updated version of the 'old' book, written by a slightly older author.

***

EVEN though this is a second edition, I must still thank all those who gave me such valuable help and assistance when writing the first edition, and I now include those who have given me additional help since. So, first and foremost, my grateful thanks to Michael Thomas and Barbara (Bobby) Perry, Patricia Roc's son and sister, for the unstinting help answering my many questions and providing me with a lot of candid and unpublished photographs. Also, Patrick Jardin and his brother Dr. Prosper Jardin in France, who spoke quite openly about Patricia Roc's time spent in Paris with her second husband, André Thomas.

An especially important part of my research was provided by those who granted me interviews or exchanged letters and telephone calls: Dame Vera Lynn, Peggy Cummins, Julie Harris, Peter Byrne, Roland Curram, Eric Smith, Jim Simpson, Dr. Melanie Bell, Muriel Pavlow, Nora Neumann, Hilton Tims and Pauline Fletcher. I must also thank Henry Jaremko who allowed me to quote from his interview with Patricia Roc, which can be found in full on his dedicated web site www.patriciaroc.com.

Over many months, the staff at the British Film Institute research library provided helpful assistance and suggestions as I trawled my way through volumes of documents and books. Similarly, I am especially grateful for the help of Sandra Archer at the Margaret Herrick Library of the Academy of Motion Picture Arts and Science, Los Angeles. A special thank you to Alison Martin at ITV Global Entertainment for letting me read the Patricia Roc files in the J. Arthur Rank archives. Also, my thanks to the City of Westminster Archives Centre, and the staff at my local library in Bradford on Avon.

The amount of help and encouragement Royal Biographer and entertainments journalist Michael Thornton gave me cannot be measured in words. Allowing me to quote extensively from the interview he did with Patricia Roc in 1995, as well as supplying me with several photographs of her, contributed greatly my understanding of the lady, and to the publication of the book you are now holding.

I owe a great deal to friends and colleagues, in particular Brian Twist who has supplied me with several photographs for this edition, Ann Kirkham, Audrey Scott and especially Judith Rider who helped extensively with the research of the Patricia Roc's films.

For neither the first time nor the last time, I dedicate a book to my wife, Sue. Her patience and humour enliven every day; her devoted support in everything I do makes all my efforts possible and worthwhile.

Patricia Roc outside St. Paul's Cathedral (Courtesy of Michael Thornton)

Introduction

SOMETHING quite extraordinary happened on the steps of St Paul's Cathedral one sunny afternoon in June 1995. As the guests were leaving the memorial service for Fred Perry, arguably Britain's greatest and certainly most successful tennis player to date, who died whilst he was in Australia in February of that year, an eighty-year old lady was besieged by fans and well wishers who remembered her when she was one of the most loved British film stars of the post war days. Still looking graceful and chic, with visibly distinct signs of the beauty she was all those years before, stood Patricia Roc surrounded by more than two hundred people, so many that two City of Westminster policemen came over to try and enforce some sort of control.

The fact that the tennis greats of the day, stars like Pete Sampras and Martina Navratilova were spilling out of the Cathedral seemed not to matter. It was Pat who they had come to see, and who patiently signed autographs and chatted to the fans for well over half-an-hour.

Journalist Quentin Letts, writing in the *Daily Telegraph* that she would be at Westminster Abbey for the memorial service of her brother-in-law Fred Perry, had alerted her fans of her arrival. Although he got the venue wrong, it did not deter them one iota – they still found her. One lady was heard to say, "I wondered if I would recognise her after all this time, but I did. She was looking as lovely as ever."

The 1940s was a 'golden age' for British female stars, with Patricia Roc one of the most popular. In her hey-day she was without doubt a phenomenon of the time, and had the rare talent of making her audience believe in her whenever she was on the screen. Her popularity - at the height of her career she was receiving more than 5000 fan letters a week - was all down to her sincerity which stood out in all her film work. She was a woman with whom the female

11

population of Britain, especially during the war years, could readily identify, and was such a class act that she would make everyone feel comfortable in her presence.

Yet behind that ethereal screen persona was a woman of immense passion with a prodigious track record with the opposite sex. Not for nothing was she dubbed 'bedrock' by the film technicians with whom she worked. Her lovers included the rich and famous including Ronald Reagan who was very much in love with her and in 1949 begged her to marry him, a proposal she turned down partly because she didn't want to spend the rest of her life in America.

***

Pat's career started in the late 1930s, spanned the 1940s and 1950s, and eventually came to a halt in the early 1960s. During that time she made forty films in Britain, Hollywood, France and Italy, and a handful of television programmes. Pat, as she liked to be called by everyone, from tea-boy to top stars and directors, may not have achieved the level of endearing fame of the Hollywood stars of the cinema, but for a comparatively brief period in the 1940s she was a big star and a huge box office attraction.   By her own admission, Pat had her limitations, telling the *Sunday Express* in 1959, "I know I'm not a great actress, I never was, but I can cope happily with most parts liable to come my way." Yet to many, she was a great star and a most beautiful woman, completely unpretentious and always full of fun. Her freshness of appeal and straightforward sincerity in even the most improbable situations were as marked as those of the sunny young soprano Deanna Durbin with whom she was frequently compared, and on occasions, mistaken for. She was always a hard working actress who tried her best to give a good performance. "I owe it to the people who indirectly pay my wages to do my best," she said. And although her 'best' may not always have found favour with the critics, who often accused her of lacking depth and emotion in her performances, the British cinemagoers loved her.

Her early film roles were usually in 'B' films, films that didn't warrant serious criticism. It wasn't until she played the coveted role of Celia, the little aircraft factory girl in Gainsborough's film *Millions Like Us* in 1943 that she broke through into major box-office stardom. Her success in that film led to a seven-year contract with Gainsborough, and to movie mogul J. Arthur Rank describing her as 'the archetypal British beauty, *the goddess of the Odeons*'.

This biography doesn't try to explain why Pat lived the life she did. Being a very private person who kept her non-professional life very much to herself, only she really knew that. It does however, endeavour to say how she lived it, and with whom.

'Baby Felicia' a few weeks old (Courtesy of Michael Thomas)

CHAPTER ONE

Growing Up

FELICIA Miriam Ursula Herold, who became Patricia Roc - *the goddess of the Odeons,* was born on 7 June 1915 at 75 Lissenden Mansions, in Lissenden Gardens, a block of flats bordering Hampstead Heath. For years Pat fibbed about her age, claiming to be three years younger than she actually was, and even today, her year of birth is still quoted as 1918 in many of the Patricia Roc website biographies. Perhaps she though that at 22, when she started out as a budding actress, that she was a little old to be making her debut. She may well have been right when you consider that Margaret Lockwood, a year younger than her, and somebody who would become one of her contemporaries and closest friends in the future, had by 1937 been in fourteen films and had already made a name for herself. Following Lockwood's appearance in Carol Reed's *The Beloved Vagabond* with Maurice Chevalier, the *Daily Sketch* hailed her as 'definitely one of our coming stars'. It would be several years before Pat would get the same sort of recognition.

On Pat's birth certificate it states that her parents were Felix Herold and his wife Miriam Muriel Herold (neé Angell) - she latter transposed her two Christian names and was always known as Muriel. In fact Felix and Muriel were not married, the falsehood no doubt fabricated to bring Felicia into the world as legitimate, or perhaps to protect Muriel's reputation, an important consideration in those days. Very little is known about Felix other than he was a paper merchant and was probably one of the 150,000 refugees who fled from Eastern Europe to Britain in the early 1900s, settling, as many did, in the Hampstead district. Whether the Lissenden Mansions address was his home or

Muriel's has never been established, but when she registered her daughter's birth a month later that is the address she gave.

Number seventy-five was one of the rented flats in a red brick block built by the Armstrong family in 1907. It is said that the family had a benign relationship with their tenants, allocating flats to children who were outgrowing their parents, to a person who might have been kicked out of a broken relationship, even letting families with dogs rent a flat with a garden. So it is quite conceivable that the Armstrongs were sympathetic to Felix and Muriel's circumstances and allocated them a flat to live in as a couple.

***

Muriel was born in St. Helier, Jersey in 1894. She was one of ten children, two boys; James and Robert, and eight girls; Elizabeth, Grace, Ann, Beatrice, Alice, Florence, Muriel and Naomi. Their parents were Frederick and Louisa Angell, both Channel Islanders having been born and raised in Jersey. Frederick Angell was a gas fitter by trade, although he had been 'elevated' to civil engineer status on one of Muriel's subsequent marriage certificates. When he died in 1904, aged 53, Louisa was left to cope with the children on her own. It must have been an arduous struggle for her because it wasn't long after her husband's death that she died. Inevitably the siblings split up. Muriel, who was now thirteen-years-old, went to stay with her older sister Grace, who had married a Company Secretary, and was living in West Kensington, London. After completing her schooling, Muriel joined a local hospital as a nurse. Soon after that, she met, and had an affair with Felix Herold.

It seems very unlikely that Felix Herold had much contact with his daughter after she was born because it wasn't him who Pat thought of as her father, but André Riese, a wealthy stockbroker born 10 December 1887 in Holland. Pat's mother used to claim that Felix had been killed whilst serving in WW1, but that seems to have been a convenient dodge to cover up the true facts. No record of a Felix Herold ever joining the armed forces, let alone being killed, exists. He simply disappeared and nothing has been heard of him since. There are no official records to show that he died, so he may well have returned to his country of origin or emigrated perhaps to America. Whatever the circumstances, it remains one of those mysteries that will probably never be solved.

It was more likely that Felix and Muriel split up shortly after Pat was born and, unable to support her daughter on her own, Muriel gave permission for her close friend André to adopt Pat and bring her up as Felicia Riese. Because adoption records didn't officially start until 1927 it is impossible to say when this was, but it has always been claimed that Pat was still an infant at the time. For many years, or so she claimed, Pat was kept in the dark about her true parentage. It wasn't, she said, until she was thirty-four and needed her birth certificate to marry Frenchman André Thomas that she discovered the truth. But if Pat was confused by the news that Felix was her real father, it didn't seem to faze her. André had always shown nothing but love towards his adopted daughter, and she in return, adored him.

André Riese was considered to be one of the most eligible bachelors in London. He was reasonably handsome, very wealthy and lived in the fashionable Portman Mansions in Marylebone. He would have been a catch for any woman, but not it seems for Muriel – not for the time being at least. She had her eyes set on Charles Henry Francis (Karl Henrick Franz) Richter, a forty-three year old Swiss manufacturing chemist, whom she married on 27 April 1918 at the Eglise Suisse Protestant Church, just off Shaftesbury Avenue in London. More than twelve months later, Muriel gave birth to their daughter Barbara (always known to her family and friends as 'Bobby'), so the marriage certainly wasn't a hurried affair to cover up another unexpected pregnancy. This marriage however didn't last, and the couple divorced in 1921. Muriel had obviously decided that it was André Riese all along that she wanted to be with, and the following year, on 27 April, they quietly married at the Marylebone Register Office in London. She was now twenty-seven and André thirty-four.

It seems extraordinary that Pat, who would have been approaching seven at the time, didn't question why her mother and the man she regarded as her father were only just getting married. Most seven-year-olds would surely have wondered what the heck was going on, and one can only speculate just how Pat's mother explained it all to her.

A year after they married, Muriel and André had a daughter, Marie-Louise. So now there were three girls in the family, each with a different father. Not that it mattered to them. Brought up by Muriel and André, the three girls,

17

Marie-Louise, 'Bobby', who became the fourth wife of British tennis ace Fred Perry, and Pat, known fondly throughout her life as 'Bunny' by the family and close friends, were devoted to one another and remained close throughout their lives. "We always said my sisters took after mum who was born in Jersey and was half French and had a little Spanish in her. They all had dark hair. Me, I was the one with light coloured hair," recalled Pat on one of the rare occasions she spoke about her mother.

Two year-old Pat with her mother (Courtesy of Michael Thomas)

As a young school girl Pat was showing signs, with her large brilliant indigo blue eyes, fringed hair and well defined, slightly chubby features, that she was going to grow up to be a real beauty – not unlike her mother. She described her childhood as being *normal* and loved school. As it was, her formative years were very much in the upper-class mould, living first in a large house in Maida Vale before moving to a large seven bedroomed house in much sought after Hamilton Terrace, Swiss Cottage.

A wealthy man, André could well afford live in servants to look after the family. There was a butler, cook, parlour maid, chauffeur and two nannies for the three girls. Life for Pat it would seem was anything but 'normal'.

Pat first attended a local prep school before going on to the all-girls prestigious Francis Holland School, at Clarence Gate, adjacent to Regent's Park. It was the school, which at different times, was attended by sisters Joan and Jackie Collins, and the comedienne Joyce Grenfell. Each morning, dressed in her grey blazer, grey felt hat and pink and white candy striped dress, the chauffeur drove Pat to school. Then, in the afternoon he would go to the school and drive her home.

Francis Holland was a genteel, expensive, terribly correct Church of England day school founded by the Reverend Francis Holland in 1878, and named after him. There, the girls were expected to wear hats and white cotton gloves at all times in public, to have immaculate manners, to speak with perfect enunciation, and to eat pudding with a fork – *not* a common spoon, if you don't mind. The school song was Rudyard Kipling's 'Children's Song' from *Puck of Pook's Hill*. It was a song that ironically, Pat took rather too literally in later life. The closing verse read:

> Teach us delight in simple things,
> And Mirth that has no bitter springs;
> Forgiveness free of evil done,
> *And love to all men 'neath the sun.*

It has been said that Pat had a tendency to be something of a tomboy but one of her classmates and best friends at school, Nora Neumann, remembered Pat as being very popular. "Felicia Riese (Pat's real name) arrived at Francis Holland School in 1925 and joined my form IIB. She very quickly made friends with everybody, and was a delightful girl, very popular with both pupils and the teachers. I remember she was tremendous fun to be with and over the years we became great friends. I visited her home on many occasions and met her parents and sisters. They went to Francis Holland too, but being much younger I didn't have anything in common with them. Felicia stayed at Francis Holland until the end of her year in the 4th Form, and then she went off to boarding school. Alas, I lost contact with her, but I certainly followed her progress in the pictures. Who would have thought that she would become a household name?" said Miss Neumann.

Pat was fourteen when her parents packed her off to the Bartram Gables Boarding School for girls in Broadstairs, Kent. For some reason, that whole area of northeast Kent was considered to be healthy, even though it was bitterly cold in the winter months, so there was an abundance of boarding schools in the area. Bartram Gables was considered to be one of the better ones. It was an oldish, but comfortable Victorian building with dormitories for around ten to twenty girls at any one time. On the wall of the dormitory where Pat slept there was a notice that read, "Ring if you require a mistress during the night". It was still there when the Royal Signals commandeered the school during the war. The soldiers frequently rang the bell, but nobody ever arrived.

***

Holiday time was always very special for Pat and her sisters. Summer holidays were spent with their parents, who invariably took them somewhere abroad – Egypt, Africa, Spain, France and many other interesting destinations that were certainly out of reach for the majority of Britons in the 1920s and 1930s. Obviously these holidays were sheer joy for Pat, Bobby and Marie-Louise, but there was an additional motive why their father chose different exotic locations to take the girls. He felt that as part of their education, they should experience first-hand different cultures and customs, and see for themselves some of the hardships some people had to endure. Christmas was always spent at home as a family but immediately afterwards, Muriel would take the girls skiing in Switzerland, always staying in one of the private suites at the Tschuggen Grand Hotel in Arosa. All three girls were proficient skiers, Pat in particular.

Many children hate leaving home to attend boarding school, but not Pat. She was not a shy girl and soon became acclimatised to the new way of life, and made many new friends at Bartram Gables. In fact she became so popular, both with the other girls and staff alike, that she eventually became the school's head girl. She left in 1933 when she was eighteen.

"I loved those four years at Bartram Gables," said Pat. "I think it was where I first became aware of acting. I remember when I was in one of the school plays thinking that this is quite exciting. But I never dreamt at the time that I would go on to be an actress, let alone a successful one, if that's what I became," she added with a wry smile. She enjoyed her indoor lessons and outdoor games in this popular Kentish seaside resort, and took part in most of the sports activities.

As well as swimming, lacrosse, tennis, and netball, riding was one of the activities encouraged by the school and Pat soon became an accomplished horsewoman. This was to prove very useful during her film career when she got to ride her own horse, 'Wallaby', in two of Gainsborough's highly successful costume dramas, The *Wicked Lady* and *Jassy,* and which, in 1937, got her a part as an extra in her very first film, *The Divorce of Lady X.* "I happened to be on the set, I wasn't there as an extra, but they asked me if I would consider doing some riding in the film because I used to ride a great deal and they wanted a competent horsewoman, so that's what I did. I wasn't there looking for a part or anything, I just happened to be in the right place at the right time," she explained. The film was made at the Denham Studios in Buckinghamshire during the summer of 1937, when Pat was actively looking for work as an actress. So, in spite of what she said, it is more than likely that she was *looking for a part*. Film sets are not the sort of places that you can wander on and off unless you are invited to do so.

The Divorce of Lady X stared Laurence Olivier, Ralph Richardson and Merle Oberon, the actress who, throughout her life, tried to hide the fact that she was of Welsh/Indian parentage, even to the extent of pretending her Indian mother was her maid. Blink and you could very well miss Pat's contribution, or, as the Americans like to call it, 'a popcorn role', so called because, when you look down to see how much popcorn you still had in the bag, you would miss seeing her. For the alert ones, Pat can be seen resting against a pillar in one scene, and in another she is riding in the hunt. Both very brief, but like she said, "It was a start."

Apart from being a good horsewoman, Pat was also an accomplished artist and whilst at Bartram Gables she painted a mural over the chapel door, which remained there until the building was demolished in the 1960s. In fact she originally wanted to be an artist, but according to her, whilst she was an excellent copyist she lacked original artistic ideas, so decided that it would be a waste of time pursuing that particular ambition. It was with some sadness, confessed Pat, when the time came to leave the boarding school, but new challenges were on the horizon.

There was a time when parents, at least those among the moneyed classes, sent their daughters to a traditional French Finishing School. Not knowing quite what to do with Pat after she left Bartram Gables – she showed little inclination for any sort of occupational vocation – this is what André and Muriel decided to do. So off went Pat to Mlle. Boutron's Finishing School for Young Ladies, in Paris, where she would learn, if she didn't already know, an irreproachable foundation in all aspects of social etiquette, entertaining and lifestyle appreciation.

As an eighteen-year-old Pat was very striking. Boys naturally were attracted to her, and she quickly cultivated a flirtatious response. Consequently, Muriel was afraid for her 'little girl' all alone in Paris of all places. But she needn't have worried. Mlle. Boutron did all she could to see that the girls behaved themselves, and didn't succumb to the delights of the Parisian nightlife. The 'school', a large five-story building in the tree-lined rue George Berger in the centre of Paris, was the proper place for wealthy young ladies to live in the 1930s. Each girl had her own palatial room overlooking *la rue*, but they had their meals together in a splendid ornate dining room. Mlle. Boutron let the girls have some freedom, but she did not allow men in the house after 10 pm, and most certainly never in the girls' living quarters. That's not to say however that the girls didn't go to a man's flat from time to time.

Having been away at boarding school for four years, then immediately whisked off to France, one would have thought that Pat would have enjoyed some time at home with her parents and sisters, but no, with her mother and father's blessing she toured France during the holiday breaks. Negotiating dusty roads by bicycle and car, searching out quaint places of interest, and loving every moment of it, Pat was in her element. By now she could speak French fluently and learnt to love France – the *bonhomie* of its inhabitants, the exotic smells of the perfume salons, the bleak wildness of parts of the country, and most of all, the Frenchman's infinite appreciation of the arts. She also fell under the spell of French films and it was at this stage in her life that she felt the definite urge to act. She wanted, she said, to become the theatrical torchbearer of her family. But her thoughts weren't on the cinema; she wanted to become a stage actress.

Pat finally returned home from France in time to spend Christmas with the family, and of course, go skiing with her mother and sisters in the New Year. When it came to her future plans her parents asked her if she had decided what she wanted to do. Oh yes, she knew all right. Instinctively she said without hesitation, "I want to become an actress." According to her sister Bobby, their father's initial reaction was one of outrage. In typical fashion he stormed, "No daughter of mine is going on the stage." He knew well enough that acting was a hard life, and at best, a precarious profession plagued with disappointments. But he was sufficiently astute to understand that his daughter knew what she was about, and it would serve no useful purpose to try and discourage her in her chosen ambition if her mind was made up. He 'gracefully', if that is the right word, gave in. But he also knew that if she wanted to learn about the theatre and acting she would have to have lessons, and what better place to get them than the Royal Academy of Dramatic Art (RADA), regarded as one of the most famous and prestigious drama schools in the world, and one of the oldest in England.

Getting into RADA where so many of Britain's leading actors and actresses learnt their trade wasn't cheap, and it wasn't easy either. Before being accepted there was a stiff entrance exam, and a tough audition to get through, and for every three applicants there was only one place available. Pat, a little apprehensive, set off one January morning with her father to the Royal Academy in Gower Street, just off Tottenham Court Road, for her audition. "I remember being a little nervous at the time and goodness knows what I read for my audition, but whatever it was impressed Sir Kenneth Barnes, the principal at the time," said Pat.

Just how she managed to break into such an exclusive acting school without, if you discount a small role in a school play, ever having performed in a single theatrical production remains a mystery, but she must have managed to convince Sir Kenneth, or 'Granny Barnes' as the students used to call him, that she was acting material, because he offered her one of the much-coveted available places. One person who failed to gain a place at the Academy that year was Frankie Howerd, who was to become one of Britain's best-loved comedians and comic actors.

André, Pat's father, was as amazed as Pat when he heard the news that his daughter had passed her audition, but he was also immensely proud and gave her his full support. So, with *daddy* paying the fees, on 1 April 1934, together with several other hopefuls, including Noele Gordon, star of the popular TV soap opera *Crossroads*, Pat entered the Academy, and set out on her long road to eventual stardom. She told her mother and father, "At last I'm really going to do what I've always wanted to do," forgetting that it was only during the previous few months she spent in Paris, that she actually got the urge to become an actress.

At RADA, pupils were told from day one that before they set foot on a stage they had to learn to walk correctly, talk posh, but with unaffected accent, and how to breathe all over again. It was basic training for theatre and a rebirth for anyone who wanted a new start in life. Students were also taught the art of applying makeup, how to open the door and enter a room gracefully, how to sit down and get up again, how to walk up and down the stairs, how to get in and out of a car without the girls showing their knickers, how to put on a pair of gloves, even how to smoke a cigarette which, in the 1930s, was not only sociably acceptable but encouraged. For somebody who had spent a year at a French finishing school, these disciplines came naturally to Pat. Students were also encouraged to study plays by Shakespeare, Marlow, Johnson and Shaw, and to go to the theatre as often as possible. The latter requirement particularly appealed to Pat.

Studying at RADA was generally a two-year course, but Pat left after completing just nine months without graduating. This meant that she was not eligible to audition for the Academy's annual production, in those days a single performance held at a West End theatre in front of theatre producers and agents who were scouting for new up and coming talent. According to Pat, she felt that she would learn more if she were to join a theatre group. What she wanted, she said, was practical experience. Acting didn't come naturally to her, and her tutors at the RADA agreed that if she were to succeed in the theatre it would be more beneficial if she joined an established drama group. In other words, she was wasting her time studying at RADA. She was naturally disappointed when she had to leave, but, for all his earlier misgivings, her father had faith in her and was now keen to see his daughter succeed. With his help, Pat became a member of the Stock Exchange Dramatic and Operatic Society (SEDOS), a society whose members have in the past included Anna Neagle who danced in the chorus as Marjorie Robertson, Guy Middleton and Rosalie Crutchley.

For several weeks Pat helped out by painting scenery, something she was particularly good at, and doing odd jobs behind the scenes before eventually appearing on stage in the company's productions: *Mr. Cinders*, *The Late Christopher Bean*, *Theatre Royal*, *Good Night Vienna*, *Ten Minute Alibi* and *Rainbow*

Inn were just some of the plays in which she played both small and larger parts.

From being a member of a small repertory company to getting work on the West End stage was a difficult transition for any actor, and a tour of the London theatrical managers proved a fruitless experience for Pat. "I was just a young hopeful; no one had heard of me or was prepared to act as my sponsor," she said.

It was at this point that she decided to return to Paris and try her luck there. She met up with old friends and, through a contact of her father, got an introduction to french film producer Edouard Cornelion-Molinier who promised to do what he could to help her. Good to his word he introduced her to the Paramount owned Joinville Film Studios in the suburbs of Paris, where she was screen tested for the role of Séverine Roubaud in *The Human Beast* opposite Jean Gabin. She did the test in both French and English, which impressed the director, Jean Renoir. Unfortunately it didn't impress the studio's hierarchy. When they saw Pat on the big screen they thought she looked far too young for such a dark and dramatic role – she was twenty-two at the time – so the part went to twenty-seven-year-old French leading actress Simone Simon.

Simone Simon was somewhat of a legend in France. When she died in 2005 aged 94, the French Cultural Minister, Renaud Donnedieu de Vabres, issued a statement in which he extolled Simone's charm and her irresistible smile. "In her passing," he said, "We have lost one of the most seductive and most brilliant stars of the French cinema." She never married, but her maid revealed that she used to reward men, to whom she took a fancy, with a gold key to her boudoir. Included was American composer and pianist George Gershwin. Pat and Simone never met during those early days in Paris, but twelve years later, when Pat moved to France, they became very good friends.

CHAPTER TWO

The Duke and the Princess

LOSING out to Simon, Pat returned to England a little disconsolate but vowed not to give up on the idea of becoming an actress. Still living at home with her parents, she returned to SEDOS and continued to bang on producers doors in the hope that one day, one of them would cast her in one of their plays. Eventually her luck was to change, as was her name, when she met the West End Theatre producer, Sydney Carroll, not by 'banging on his door', but through her *inamorato*. At the time, Pat was spending a lot of time with the Duke of Rutland and his family, whom she got to know through her friendship with Lady Isobel Manners, the 9th Duke of Rutland's daughter, who was at Mlle. Boutron's Finishing School in Paris at the same time Pat was there. Frequently, Pat would spend her weekends at Belvoir Castle, the seat of the Dukes of Rutland for over three centuries, where she would often go foxhunting with the family.

According to Pat's sister Bobby, Pat struck up a close relationship with the fifty-three-year-old Duke. "He took her out to dinner many times, and Oh! she didn't come home those evenings either," chuckled Bobby mischievously. It was a relationship that Pat's father didn't altogether approve of, and understandably, seeing he was a couple of years younger than the Duke. But his daughter was of an age, she was 22, when she could please herself who she went out with, and did so, especially if it helped with her career. It was during one of 'those evenings', dining at the Savoy Grill, when the Duke introduced her to Sydney Carroll, an introduction that proved to be the stepping-stone Pat had been hoping for, for some time.

Carroll was pretty astute and had an eye for talent, starting many aspiring youngsters on the road to fame. Vivien Leigh was given her first big opportunity on the London stage when Carroll spotted her working in the provinces. He cast her in *The Mask of Virtue* at The Ambassadors Theatre, which he managed, and she never looked back. He also 'discovered' Margaret Lockwood in 1934 and gave her a small part in *Family Affairs*. When he met Pat that evening he could see that she had potential, but he had reservations. There was little doubt that he was impressed with her looks, but her lack of acting experience and the fact that she had not completed the full two years at RADA, as Margaret Lockwood for instance had, worried him a little. However, he promised to do what he could. Within days he contacted Pat and offered her a part in Guy Bolton's comedy, *Nuts in May,* which Carroll was putting on at the Ambassadors Theatre. Pat jumped with glee when she heard the news and relished the thought of playing Miss Clark, a smouldering secretary in the play.

There was just one slight problem and that was Pat's name. Carroll thought that Felicia Riese sounded a little foreign and a little characterless. In order to project the right image he suggested that she change her name completely. What she needed, he told her, was a short name, one which people would remember without too much difficulty. He first suggested Ann Kent, presumably because Pat had been to a boarding school in Kent. "Oh no, I don't think that's what I really want," she recalled. At the time there used to be the Rock Film Studios at Elstree, which, as an alternative to 'Kent', prompted Carroll to suggest 'Rock'. "Immediately I said 'yes'. That didn't sound too bad, but to make it easier still I suggested Roc without the 'k'. Then, as my first name was Felicia and could be shortened to 'Flee', *Flee Roc*, can you imagine! I chose Patricia, which is quite near to Felicia, and I didn't mind it being shortened to Pat. So, Patricia Roc I became."

One of her first duties as *Patricia Roc* was to attend her sister's wedding. Bobby was nineteen, and had met and fallen for a twenty-one year old American, Seymour Friedman, who came to England to be educated at Cambridge and then St Mary's Hospital Medical School. Abandoning his medical studies, he became interested in the film industry and got a job with Columbia Pictures in Hollywood as an assistant editor. Within weeks of getting married, he whisked Bobby off to America, where she has lived ever since, but not with Seymour; they divorced in the 1940s. The whole family, Pat in particular, tried to dissuade Bobby from marrying at such a young age and going off to live thousands of miles away from her family, but Bobby liked Seymour enough to take that chance. Following her divorce from Seymour, Bobby became the fourth wife of Britain's tennis ace, Fred Perry.

"Here we come gathering nuts in May:" We know it looks more as though they're collecting kisses ... but "Nuts in May" is the title of the play they appear in—it's at the Ambassadors Theatre, London.

Enraptured couple are Patricia Roc and Steve Geray . . "Come on, Steve!"

(Daily Express 7 February 1938)

Nuts in May opened in the West End at the Ambassadors Theatre on 3 February 1938. The sixpenny programme, illustrated by the cartoonist Vicky, listed the performers as Magda Kun, Hugh Dempster, Rosamund Greenwood, Steve Geray, Peter Haddon, Kate Cutler, Naya Grecia and Patricia Roc in that order. It also reminded the patrons that smoking was not permitted in the auditorium, whilst an advertisement celebrated State Express cigarettes (1/4d. for 20, which is about 7p in today's money) as 'Perfection'. Pat loved the whole ambiance of the theatre and was happy in the knowledge that she had 'arrived' in the West End, and settled down to enjoy a long run, or so she thought.

The play revolves around the scatty Baroness Prischky, played by Magda Kun, who rips out pages of a book as she reads them, writes letters and envelopes then destroys them, and mistakes her doctor, played by Peter Haddon, for her husband. Steve Geray plays Baron Prischky her husband who, in the last act, kisses and cuddles Patricia Roc his secretary, as she sits crossed legged (and showing a lot of it) on the piano. It was a rather silly adaptation of A. Benedetti's comedy by Guy Bolton, Sonny Miller and Geray, which received such poor notices that it closed after four weeks. "After two acts, the play ceased to amuse us by whatever humour it possessed and steadfastly refused to move forward by so much as an inch," wrote John Grime in the *Daily Express* 4 February 1938.

Rosamund Greenwood, who played the part of the maid, Millie, described Pat as having instant sex appeal. "The moment she walked onto the stage, every man in the audience sat up and took notice," she told Royal Biographer and entertainments journalist, Michael Thornton. Pat's 'appeal' also caught the attention of the Hungarian immigrant movie mogul of the 1930s and 1940s, Alexander Korda, who attended her opening- night performance, and arranged for her to have a screen test. Korda, who had a keen eye (and a warm bed) for a pretty girl no doubt remembered Pat from the time she was an extra in his film *The Divorce of Lady X*. But whether he did or not, the outcome of the test was that Pat was given the role of a Polish princess in Korda's 1938 costume epic *The Rebel Son*. Apart from *The Divorce of Lady X*, it was the first of forty films Pat made during her acting career.

The Rebel Son, based on Nikolai Gogol's story Taras Bulba, tells the tale of the 16th-century Cossack leader, played by Harry Baur, and his two sons Peter a fighter, and Andrei a student. Taras sends Andrei to study their Polish rulers and gather information to learn how the Cossacks can overthrow the Poles in battle. The plan backfires when the Andrei falls in love with Princess Marina played by Patricia Roc, the daughter of a Polish nobleman and sworn enemy of Taras.

The French first filmed the story with the title *Taras Bulba* in 1936. It did well enough on the continent to prompt Korda to commission an English-language version with a new title *The Cossack*, later changed to *The Rebel Son*. The trouble was that the film's director Adrian Brunel, whose career peaked during the silent film era, used generous portions of footage from the 1936 French version directed by Alexis Granowsky, resulting in a mishmash of contrasting styles. Not only that, but some additional scenes directed by an uncredited Albert de Coureville, bore little relation to Brunel's work. Little wonder the critics were bemused and quick to pass unfavourable judgment on the picture. Trade magazine, *Monthly Film Bulletin,* felt that the acting was uneven and that the English players were quite unlike Cossacks. Even more damning, the astringent critic of the day, Graham Green, when he reviewed the film for the London *Evening Standard* wrote, "A man in the audience was remarking slowly with some of Dr. Johnson's weight, 'I am wondering what the reason of the existence of this film can be'." Pat, on the other hand, acquitted herself well in her first film. She could console herself with the fact that the critics didn't mock her performance. "Patricia Roc as Princess Marina is the only one who seems at home in her part," wrote the *Catholic News* critic *in* September 1939.

Made at Korda's Denham film studios, the entire cast and crew went out of their way to welcome Pat in her first film role, especially Anthony Bushell who played Taras' son Andrei. He was to give Pat her very first screen kiss, which in turn led to a brief romance away from the set. Born in Westerham, Kent, and educated at Oxford, Bushell appeared on Broadway in the late 1920s and made several films in Hollywood before returning to England in 1932 with his wife, American musical comedy star Zelma O'Neal, whom he married in 1928 and divorced in 1935. After serving in the army during the war, during which time he met and married his second wife Ann, Bushell returned to acting and also moved to the production side of the business, forming a close personal and business relationship with Laurence Olivier. It was the only film he and Pat were to make with one another.

Roger Livesey, who played the other son Peter, came to prominence in 1943 when he took the lead in the Michael Powell's film, *The Life and Death of Colonel Blimp.* But it was Harry Baur, one of the most distinguished character actors in Europe during the 1930s, who was the star of *The Rebel Son.* . However, with the advent of the war and Hitler, Baur learned that stardom was no cushion against fascisms. In 1942, whilst in Berlin to star in his last film *Symphone eines Lebens*, Baur's Jewish wife was arrested on a trumped-up espionage charge. His efforts to secure her release led to his own arrest and torture at the hands of the Gestapo. In April 1943 the Germans made a show of releasing him from prison but a few days later he was found dead in Paris in mysterious circumstances. "His death was a travesty," said Pat. "He was so kind to me when I was making that picture; I will never forget him."

At a time in Hollywood when spectacular block-busters like *The Ten Commandments* and *Ben Hur* were the money making trend, United Artists remade the Gogol classic, *Taras Bulba*, in 1962. But even though the cast included Yul Brynner and Tony Curtis, it fared little better than Brunel's attempt. It did however receive an Oscar nomination for the best musical score.

Having completed her first picture, Pat started planning for a busy future. Alexander Korda had given the inexperienced Pat some valuable advice. "At this stage in your career, do as many pictures as you can," he told her.

Pat heeded Korda's advice and with his help plunged into a series of indifferent pictures. "In those days you learnt your job by working and doing as many of the 'B' pictures as possible. I was a freelance actress and took anything offered me. Now, today, people just do something on television and they think they are stars. In my day it was hard graft, I can tell you," said Pat in 2003 during one of the last interviews she gave.

Outside Mlle. Boutron's Parisian Finishing School in 1934: Pat on the left, with her 'class-mates'. Next to Pat; Nancy, Mlle. Boutron, Iris, Lady Isobel Manners and Rosemary (Courtesy of Michael Thomas)

CHAPTER THREE

Learning Her Trade in the 'B' Pictures

GENERALLY, the term 'B' picture referred to a film that was intended for distribution as the less-publicised bottom half of a double feature, and invariably had running times of 70 minutes or less. Instinctively, the term suggested that they were inferior to the more handsomely budgeted headliners, and were frequently ignored by the major critics. But from their beginnings to the present day, 'B' movies have provided opportunities for those coming up in the profession. Celebrated filmmakers such as Anthony Mann, learned their craft in 'B' pictures by directing low-budget assignments, and actors such as John Wayne and Jack Nicholson became established by starting off in 'B' pictures. Pat was in good company.

Tipped off by an agent that there was a gorgeous new actress just starting in the business, film producer Michael Balcon was persuaded to take a look at Pat. He liked what he saw and cast her in *The Gaunt Stranger*. It was the first of many 'B' pictures she made during the early days of her career. It was also the first picture Balcon produced for Ealing Studios after defecting from Metro Goldwym Mayo, to become the head of Ealing in 1938.

The Gaunt Stranger was an adaptation of an Edgar Wallace mystery classic already popular in stage and previous screen versions. The story is about a well-known criminal lawyer, Maurice Meister (played by Wilfrid Lawson) who receives a death threat from a mysterious killer and master of disguise known only as The Ringer. He holds Meister responsible for the death of his sister. Scotland Yard detective, Inspector Alan Wembury (played by Patrick Barr) and Dr. Lomond, (brilliantly played by the distinguished Canadian actor, Alexander Knox) a police psychologist, unite to find The Ringer before he can carry out his threat. Needless to say, and in spite of a heavy police protection squad, The Ringer, whom it transpires is Dr. Lomond in disguise, carries out his threat, murders Meister, and escapes. An element of comedy was introduced in the film with the inclusion of Jessie Matthews' husband, Sonnie Hale, a thief doing time in one of His Majesty's prisons, but who is let out to help find The Ringer because he is the only one who has ever seen him face to face.

As one would expect from Michael Balcon, the finished product was a reliable thriller, and arguably better than an earlier version filmed in 1931 with the title, *The Ringer*. Balcon got Sidney Gilliat, who worked behind the scenes on the 1931 version, to script the remake. Gilliat was not at all happy with the assignment, explaining, "In *The Gaunt Stranger* I found the terrible difficulty that something is stated to be going to happen at a certain time. Until that time comes you're either misleading the audience or just stringing them along by inventing incidents to keep it going. This becomes mechanical." Nevertheless, the cinemagoers liked the modestly priced picture. It did well at the box-office, making a small profit for Balcon. "Dialogue, humour and suspense are effectively alternated...the film is in fact capital crime fiction," wrote the critic for the trade paper *Kinematograph Weekly* in 1939.

Pat was cast as Meister's secretary Mary Lenley. It was a secondary role but she handled it with ease. According to an article in *Classic Images* in 2003, it was noted in the press that, "Patricia Roc did nicely as the heroine in *The Gaunt Stranger*". Quite unfairly, in his book *Launder and Gilliat* published in 1977, Geoff Brown wrote, "Wilfrid Lawson over acts pleasingly; Patricia Roc over acts unpleasingly." If the accusation of overacting can be levelled at anyone it must be Louise Henry who plays Cora Ann, The Ringer's wife. She weaves in and out of the plot for no apparent reason overacting outrageously as she does so.

It is easy to dismiss these hoary old thrillers of the 1930s, but under the direction of Walter Forde, regarded as one of Britain's foremost directors in the early 1930s, *The Gaunt Stranger* is well constructed through his clever use of the camera, and his masterly sound techniques. The film does however contain too many loose ends that are probably the fault of Charles Saunders, the editor. Several characters are left stranded by inconclusive plot developments. For instance, the on screen romance between Patrick Barr and Pat is left in limbo without any satisfactory explanation or conclusion. Do they or don't they make it to the altar? We will never know.

Although this was Pat's second film, it was the first that introduced her to the cinema-going public. It went on general release in December 1938, several months ahead of *The Rebel Son*, which was delayed because of post-production difficulties. The beauty spot just below the right side of Pat's mouth, which was prominent in her earlier film and early publicity pictures, had gone by the time she made *The Gaunt Stranger*. It was either removed surgically or disguised with make-up, and never to be seen again throughout her career. "I do remember having a beauty spot, and I used to darken it much the same as Maggie (Margaret Lockwood) did in *The Wicked Lady*", but it really didn't suit me half as much as it did her. I was advised to hide it, so I did," recalled Pat.

An early publicity picture of Pat taken in 1939 without beauty spot
(Author's Private Collection)

Pat's entry into the cinema and the accompanying exposure, prompted several offers of film work to come her way. Any aspirations she might have had for the theatre seemed to have dwindled as her potential to become film actress became apparent. Following *The Gaunt Stranger*, she was cast by Jack Raymond in two further Edgar Wallace stories, *The Mind of Mr Reeder* and *The Missing People*. Made by Grand National Pictures, they both starred Will Fyffe, the pawky Scots comedian, famous in the music halls for his song "I Belong to Glasgow". He played Mr Reeder, the seemingly rustic Scotland Yard detective who, like Hercule Poirot, Sherlock Holmes and other fictional detectives, always managed to solve the crimes they investigated.

Of the two, *The Missing People* was probably the better film, certainly as far as Patricia Roc was concerned. She was well down the 'pecking order' in the cast list of *The Mind of Mr Reeder*, not even having a character name, and went totally un-noticed by the critics. But she fared better in *The Missing People*. 'Patricia Roc and Ronald Shiner as the old lag, score in support', wrote the critic for *Kinematograph Weekly* in 1939

In the film she plays the part of Doris Bevan who unwittingly helps Mr. Reeder solve the mystery of a number of missing people who, it turns out, have been murdered. The missing people are individuals without friends, lived alone, and received money by post each month that stopped once they had disappeared. Reeder befriends Doris, a lonely figure, and quickly deduces that she is about to be the next victim. Like the others, she has just invested a lot of money with a firm of financial investors owned by Mr De Silvo, a mysterious man who nobody has ever seen, not even his secretary Surtees (Ronald Adams) because he, conveniently for the story, is blind. Next to Surtees' office is a firm of solicitors run by two brothers Ernest and Joseph played by Anthony Holmes and Lyn Harding. With beefy, bushy eyed browed Harding in the cast, an actor who specialized in playing villains, it is pretty obvious who is behind the disappearances.

Reeder becomes suspicious and decides to investigate the two brothers further. With this, Ernest wants to cut and run but Joseph persuades him to wait until they have dealt with Doris, Reeder and Surtees. All three are lured down to the brothers' country house where they are imprisoned in a bricked-up basement and, like all the other victims, will be drowned. The plan is thwarted when a burglar called Sam Hackett, played by Ronald Shiner, is prowling around the basement on his own 'affairs' and enables Reeder, Doris and Surtees to escape. Reeder had of course realized before going to the house that he would be walking into a trap, and arranged for the flying squad to show up and arrest the brothers.

The *Monthly Film Bulletin* gave the film the thumbs up, saying: "The cast give a sound backing to a film which grips right from the start and Will Fyffe, although perhaps falling short of some people's idea of J.G. Reeder, undoubtedly gives a fine performance as the character of Edgar Wallace".

These films, all with a running time of about 70 minutes, were the typical 'B' films of the period. They were films that Pat threw herself into with great energy and enthusiasm. "I practically lived at the studio in those days," she said. "I loved working and I was always at the studio even when I wasn't needed. I just loved it. I liked the atmosphere and I enjoyed everybody I worked with. I can't say every film was good but I was learning the whole time," she added.

***

Whenever Pat got the chance she would go (as suggested by RADA) to the theatre to see as many West End productions as possible. To say she adored the theatre would be putting it mildly. Consequently, she saw many of the great actors of the day performing on stage. One of those was Michael Redgrave whom she admired greatly, never thinking that one day she would play opposite him. But that is what she did when she was cast as his long-suffering wife in *A Window in London*. Pat was billed fifth beneath Michael Redgrave, Paul Lucas, Sally Gray and Hartley Power. She didn't have a very large part in the film, but what she did do she did well. It was probably her best acting role to date, and gave her the chance to inject a bit of characterization into her part which didn't go unnoticed. The *Monthly Film Bulletin* for instance commented that; "Patricia Roc gives a charming little character study of a working girl wife."

In *A Window in London*, Pat, whose character name is also Pat, works nights as a telephonist at a large block of flats, whilst her husband Peter (Michael Redgrave) works in the day as a crane operator, working on the new Waterloo Bridge in London. Consequently they see very little of one another. One morning as Peter is on his way to work, he sees what he thinks is a *crime passionel* from the window of the train. He later returns with a police officer to the flats where he thinks a murder has taken place, but discovers it was only an ageing stage magician, Zoltini (Paul Lucas) a highly volatile and jealous man, and his attractive wife-turned-assistant Vivienne (Sally Gray) rehearsing an illusion. Peter and Vivienne strike up a friendship, which Zoltini takes exception to, certain that the couple are having an affair. After a few twists and turns, Zoltini shoots his wife. Meanwhile, Pat has found a day job and she and Peter are romantically reunited.

Herbert Mason the director, a nephew of the great Shakespearian actress Ellen Terry, was really a man of the theatre, but emerged unexpectedly as a director of several major British pictures in the late 1930s. Considered to be one of his more interesting films, *A Window in London* was a dark and disturbing remake of Maurice Cam's French circular drama *Métropolitain*, released in February 1939. The feeling of faint unease that Mason engenders throughout is very skilfully done, even though the *New York Times* critic felt that the film, re-titled *Woman in Distress* for the American market, and cut from its original running time of 76 minutes by 8 minutes, was 'muddily photographed and poorly directed'. The central plot was later used for the American Oscar nominated comedy *Hiss and Yell* (1946).

Even though Pat and Sally Gray, a year older and known for her attractive husky voice, didn't have any scenes together in the film, they became good friends up until the time Sally Gray secretly became the third wife of 4th Lord Oranmore and Browne in 1951, and cut herself off from acting completely. "She was a lovely girl, a really lovely girl. I was sorry when we lost touch with one another," said Pat. *Variety*, the American entertainment trade paper and show business bible, picked out both women in their review; 'Sally Gray and Patricia Roc photograph nicely with the latter more impressive in the femme division."

Whilst Michael Redgrave was totally miscast and failed to convince as 'your average working-class Londoner', Paul Lucas stole every scene he was in. "Paul was really good company and very kind to me. He more or less took me under his wing, and I learnt a lot from him. Not like Michael who seemed to have little time for me; what a disappointment he turned out to be," recalled Pat with some regret. Born in Hungary in 1895, Paul Lucas was a leading actor in his own country before going to Hollywood in the late 1920s. He appeared in a number of films, including *Watch on the Rhine*, for which he won the Oscar in 1943 as best actor.

Pat far left with her mother and two sisters Mari-Louise and 'Bobby' in the late 1920s
(Courtesy of Michael Thomas)

Pat, 'Bobby' and Marie-Louise at the Tschuggen Club Ski Races, Arosa in 1935.
All three were proficient skiers, particularly Pat.
(Courtesy of Michael Thomas)

133 Hamilton Terrace, Swiss Cottage where Pat grew up
(Author's Private Collection)

Patricia Roc's first screen role as Princess Marina in 'The Rebel Son'.
It was the only film in which her beauty spot was ever seen
(Author's Private Collection)

'The Rebel Son' - some of the cast and crew. Patricia Roc standing behind Frederick Culley. On his right, Roger Livesey and squatting behind the clapperboard is Adrian Brunel, the film's director.
(Courtesy of Brian Twist)

Pat in 'A Window in London' 1939
(Author's Private Collection)

CHAPTER FOUR

Marriage and Michael Wilding

ON Sunday 3 September 1939, Pat was preparing to complete her last scenes in *Dr. O'Dowd*, the film she was making at the Teddington riverside studios, when, at a quarter-past eleven in the morning, British Prime Minister Neville Chamberlain, in a weary and dispirited voice, announced over the radio that a state of war existed between Britain and Germany. It looked as though the film industry would become the first casualty. Only a few weeks earlier a Home Office circular warned cinema managers that in the event of war breaking out, all cinemas as well as theatres, music halls and other places of entertainment would have to close. Shortly after Chamberlain's broadcast, a further radio announcement confirmed the order on the grounds of public safety. Film studios laid off their staff, retaining a skeleton crew to keep themselves operational and await further announcements. *Dr. O'Dowd* was temporarily abandoned.

With production at a halt, and little chance of further film work for the foreseeable future, or so it seemed at the time, Pat was effectively out of a job. Still living with her parents in Hamilton Terrace, she, like millions of others, was uncertain just what her role in the conflict would be. Should she make herself available for voluntary or military service? Her immediate response was twofold; first, wait until the situation had been clarified, and second, get married. She had known Dr. Murray Laing, a thirty-six year old Canadian, for almost nine months, having met him in the New Year when they were both on a skiing holiday in Arosa, Switzerland. The fact that he was eleven years older didn't faze her.

Tall, reasonably good-looking with a modicum of charm, Murray Laing arrived in England in October 1933 as a medical student. Four years later he qualified as an osteopath and set up a practice in London's Mayfair district.

Murray was a heavy smoker and was rarely seen without a cigarette or pipe in his hand. In Pat's eyes, this was an air of sophistication that appealed to her. But for a young woman who seemed worldly, who was well educated and came from a good background, she was in many respects really very young. Letting her heart rule her head - as she frequently did - within a month of meeting Murray the impetuous Pat announced her engagement to him. On 9 February, the *Daily Mirror* reported the announcement.

Miss Felicia (Bunny) Riese is Patricia Roc, the film actress. But her latest contract isn't the screen kind. She's engaged—to Dr. Murray R. Laing, only son of Mr. and Mrs. W. J. Laing, of Ontario, Canada.

With the outbreak of war, instead of waiting until the following year as planned, it seemed the right time for the couple to get married. Murray was living in a bachelor flat in South Audley Street, Mayfair, almost next door to St. Mark's Church, where Pat and Murray exchanged their marriage vows on Saturday 16 September. It wasn't a white wedding. Being hastily arranged there was no time to get fitted out in a traditional wedding dress. Instead, for the ceremony Pat wore a simple elegant cream coat and navy blue dress, and carried a small posy of white flowers. Neither was it a lavish affair. Apart from the family, only a few friends were invited. It has been suggested that, like many other young women, Pat rushed into marriage to avoid being called up into the armed forces, something she strenuously denied.

Pat arriving at St Mark's Church, Mayfair with her father,
for her marriage to Murray Laing in September 1939
(Courtesy of Michael Thomas)

Murray Laing – always with a cigarette
(Courtesy of Michael Thomas)

"We were in love and with the future being so uncertain, we, like lots of other couples at the time, decided not to wait any longer," she said. Whatever her reasons for getting married, the doctor, exempt from military service because of his occupation, and his bride embarked on a brief honeymoon before moving into an apartment in Eaton House, Upper Grosvenor Street, just off Park Lane in the 'swanky part' of London. In the meantime, like many in the film industry, Pat was wondering when she would be able to return to what she loved doing most of all – making pictures. "She didn't want to rivet in a factory," said her only surviving sister, Bobby, in 2008. "No," she added, "she wanted to make pictures and help the war effort that way, by entertaining the public and keeping up their morale generally."

As it was, Pat didn't have to wait very long before she was back in front of the cameras. Within a couple of weeks of the declaration of war when the anticipated enemy bombing raid failed to materialise, the cinema audiences began to get restless. The *Kinematograph Weekly* published an open plea to the government of the day:

'If intoxication is becoming a public scandal, if public houses have sold out of beer by 8p.m, just because the people will insist upon being with a crowd of their fellows and there is nowhere else to go, then the time for reopening the kinema (sic)…has become an urgent necessity.'

The government was forced to agree, allowing the 4,800 cinemas around the country, and most other places of entertainment, to re-open in the firm belief that it would boost morale on the home front, and take the minds of the population off the war for a short while at least. And the government was right; the British film-going public flocked in their millions to the cinema during the war years, a period that was to be a boom time for the film industry. Attendances steadily rose from 990 million in 1939 to a peak of 1,653 million in 1946. It didn't seem to matter how bad or indifferent the film was, there was always an enthusiastic audience ready to queue outside the cinema to see it, just to escape the realities of the war for a few hours.

Dr. O'Dowd, the picture Pat was working on when war was declared, went into production in August. Having just finished making *A Window in London*, Pat couldn't have been more delighted to be working once more with Herbert Mason who was to direct this sentimental story of lost loyalties in a small mining village. In her opinion, he was one of the best directors she had worked with, certainly in her early days as an actress.

In the film, stage and variety star Shaun Glenville plays the title role of an Irish doctor who enjoys having a drink with his working-class patients. One day he is called on to perform an emergency operation on his daughter-in-law (Pamela Wood). When she subsequently dies, the doctor's son Stephen, played by Liam Gaffney, falsely accuses his father of being drunk and negligent whilst performing the operation. As a result, he is struck off the register and retires to a remote village. However, a few years later, following an outbreak of diphtheria, his son is in desperate need of a difficult operation in order to save his life. Having lost his confidence, O'Dowd is reluctant to perform the operation, but his young granddaughter pleads with him to at least try and save her father. He performs the operation successfully, prompting his son to retract his false accusation, and the discredited old man is restored to professional honour and happiness.

Made on location in Cumbria as well as the studio, the film marked the debut of thirteen-year-old Peggy Cummins. She played O'Dowd's granddaughter. Pat played Rosemary her governess, and acquits herself admirably in the film, but it was Peggy Cummins who received most of the plaudits. Fan magazine *Picturegoer* for instance, considered that she was; "a distinct discovery and her future promises very well indeed." And her career did indeed blossom for a time.

Born in 1925 in Wales, she came to the attention of Darryl F. Zanuck, head of 20th Century Fox, who, in a blaze of publicity took her to Hollywood in the mid-1940s to star in Fox's film adaptation of the notorious Kathleen Windsor novel, *Forever Amber*. The part was first offered to Margaret Lockwood who turned it down, as did, or so it was reported, Vivien Leigh. In the early stages of shooting however, Zanuck was disappointed in Peggy's performance and rapidly replaced her with Linda Darnell. Before returning to England in 1950 to marry Derek Dunnett, Peggy Cummins made six films in America, including *Gun Crazy*, a film noir classic in which she gave an unforgettable performance as Annie Laurie Starr, a psychopathic Bonnie Parker type criminal. Her career, like that of Pat's, came to an end in the early 1960s when she decided to concentrate on her family.

"I was only young when I made *Dr. O'Dowd*, my first ever film, but I remember Pat very well. It was a time of uneasiness and I remember we used to fill sand bags in readiness of air-raid attacks when we weren't filming. We got on so well together and had lots of fun. Pat really looked after me whist we

47

were making that film. She was like a big sister," recalled Peggy Cummins. "

Dr. O'Dowd was released the following summer, but no copies appear to have survived. In fact, when, in 1992, the British Film Institute (BFI) initiated a search for some of the best-lost British films ever made, *Dr. O'Dowd* was included in the short list of ninety-two of the most sought after. Reminiscing many years later about her film career, Peggy Cummins said that she had heard that everything to do with the film was destroyed when the Teddington Studios took a direct hit from a German V1 rocket on 5 July 1944, killing three employees, including the studio manager, Doc Saloman. When Hollywood actor Danny Kaye officially opened the rebuilt studio on 28 January 1948, the administration building was named The Doc Saloman Building in his honour.

When the government cancelled its cinema closure order, *Dr. O'Dowd* was quickly completed at Teddington, before the studio shut down completely until the following summer. Only four studios; Ealing, Gainsborough, British National and Butcher, continued to operate on a regular basis during the early months of the war. Butcher's Film Services, a small production and distribution company operating at the Walton-on-Thames studios, was one of the first to resume production in October 1939 with a prison comedy, *Jailbirds*. This was quickly followed by *Pack Up Your Troubles*, one of the many 'joining up' comedies inspired by the upheaval of being conscripted into the armed services.

Whilst Pat may not have been called up during the ensuing conflict with Germany, at least she got to don an army uniform for her role in *Pack Up Your Troubles*, playing Sally Brown, a transport driver in the Auxiliary Territorial Service (ATS). In the film, Tommy Perkins played by Reginald Purdell, an actor who appeared in five pictures with Pat during her film career, joins the army at the outbreak of the war and meets up with Sally Brown. They 'fall' for one another and become engaged. Tommy is sent to France, where he and his army pal, Eric Sampson (Wylie Watson) are captured by the Germans. Following an amount of implausible comedy and ventriloquism, the two escape and are returned home. Re-united, Tommy and Sally get married with Eric as best man. The film ends with most of the main players linking arms and singing the title song 'Pack Up Your Troubles'.

Hurriedly made by Oswald Mitchell, and released in March 1940, this forgettable 'B' picture did little to further Pat's career, even though she was noticed by the critics; "Sally Brown, nick named 'Fanny' in the film, is attractively played by Patricia Roc," wrote the *Today's Cinema* critic.

One aspect of the shooting schedule that Pat wasn't at all happy with, was when she found that she had to smoke cigarettes in the film. "I don't smoke and never have, so I wasn't very keen, but it amused my younger sister Marie-Louise who, as a smoker, realised I hated it and laughed every time she saw me with a cigarette in my mouth," recalled Pat.

The production wrapped in November 1939, giving Pat and her husband time to adjust to married life. For the first time in her life she briefly assumed the role of a full-time housewife. Up until now she had been used to others looking after her every need; now it was her turn to do the housework and cook the meals. Not that the latter was a chore. Pat was an accomplished cook, a skill she had picked up during her time in France. But as for housework – "I coped," she said.

Christmas that year was spent as usual with her parents and younger sister Marie-Louise. But the customary New Year skiing holiday had to go by the board. Instead, and because Pat was still a freelance actress, she spent a good deal of her time looking for suitable film parts. Luckily, British film producer Victor Hanbury was casting for his film drama *A Gentleman of Venture,* released in October 1940 with the new title *It Happened to One Man*. Hanbury offered Pat a role opposite Nora Swinburne, and her old friend Wilfrid Lawson.

The film was based on Roland Pertwee's popular stage play, but for some reason it didn't transfer to the cinema screen very well. 'A threadbare theatrical fustian' is how the *New York Times* described the film when it reached America. Pat was cast as Betty, the daughter of Felton Quair (Wilfrid Lawson), a man who loses his fortune and his family, thanks to the chicanery of his crooked business partner, played by Reginald Tate. After spending four years in prison for fraud, Quair attempts to redeem himself but his wife Alice (Nora Swinburne) and daughter reject him.

Paul Ludwig Stein, an Austrian by birth, directed the film, which went into production in February at the Rock Studios. Stein had spent several years in America directing musicals, romances and melodramas before coming to England. Because of his Hollywood experience he was given some prestigious films to direct; this wasn't one of his best. His approach was inclined to be over-melodramatic, and he never quite made up his mind whether to concentrate on the domestic family life or the sheer adventure. As for Pat, this was one of her least favourite films.

"Patricia Roc contributes slipshod work," wrote the critic for *Variety* in 1941. It seems, for whatever reason, that Pat's heart just wasn't in this particular assignment. Possibly the old adage 'marry in haste, repent at leisure' was beginning to dawn on her. Murray's jealousy of Pat, a woman with a warm and passionate nature, rendered him insecure, possessive and well aware of her allure for other men. He had accompanied her a couple of times to see films she had made, but he wasn't at all keen on seeing his wife on the big screen. Whenever there was a love scene between Pat and another actor he became fidgety and tended to look away. He would have preferred it if she had given up acting altogether and pursued a different career – stay at home housewife perhaps. And perhaps she would have done if Murray had given her the baby she longed for. But according to her, he didn't want children, and that became a big stumbling block in their marriage, or so she said.

At this stage in her chosen career Pat was lagging behind her contemporaries in the film world. If she was aiming to become a leading player in the movies, she would soon have to make a big advance to stardom. She had made nine films to date, and was fast approaching her twenty-fifth birthday, a similar age to Margaret Lockwood who was seen as the foremost British screen actress of her generation. She, as the saying goes, had the field to herself. Others staking their claim to stardom included Valerie Hobson with over thirty films to her credit, and two years younger than Pat, Phyllis Calvert and Deborah Kerr. They had already made big impressions with the filmmakers and fans. "At first I didn't find the path of a potential film star an easy one, it was very hard work, but that made it all the more exciting and I was determined to make it," Pat was later to say. Whilst 'making it' was still some way off, she did the right thing by signing up with Eric Goodhead, an agent who was attached to Linnet and Dunfee, a prestigious theatrical agency at that time. He was to steer Pat's career to the zenith it would later achieve.

***

Pat's next film, made at the Walton-on Thames Studios, was another crime melodrama called *Three Silent Men*. She plays the daughter of a peace-loving surgeon who is accused of murdering one of his patients. Pat has the task of establishing his innocence. It was, she said, another one of her least favourite films, although she did enjoy working with handsome Derrick de Marney, the older brother of Terence de Marney, who died after falling under a train in 1971.

Three Silent Men was directed by Thomas Bentley and received reasonable press reviews; "Distinguished workmanlike characterisations by Derrick de Marney and Patricia Roc' wrote the critic for *Kinematograph Weekly* in 1940, but it was still just another 'B' film of little consequence.

A better opportunity came along in the summer of 1940 by way of *The Farmer's Wife*. Within days of finishing *Three Silent Men*, Patricia Roc went off to Welwyn in Hertfordshire, one of the few studios that was not requisitioned by the Government at the outbreak of war, to start filming this rural comedy for Associated British Picture Corporation (ABPC). The film was based on Eden Phillpotts' comic novel and stage play, and first filmed in 1928 during the silent era by Alfred Hitchcock. Basil Sydney, probably best known for his portrayal of Claudius in Laurence Olivier's 1948 Oscar winning film, *Hamlet,* plays the role of a farmer looking for a wife. Patricia Roc plays Sibley, the younger of his two daughters.

ABPC films were generally acknowledged to be second features, the quota quickies of the 1940s and 1950s. Consequently, much of the studio's output was routine and decidedly British, restricting their success outside the UK. Writing for the *New York Times' All Movie Guide,* Hal Erickson summed it up perfectly when he wrote; "*The Farmer's Wife* is a prime example of the sort of fare that struck a proper chord with British filmgoers, but whose appeal would be lost to any other nationality." He was right in as much as the British cinemagoers loved it, but could they understand what was being said? According to one critic, "Whether it was the sound recording or the exaggerated burr of the actors, it was not easy to catch all the dialogue."

Pat's co-star and love interest in the film was twenty-eight year old Michael Wilding. He was cast as the suave suitor Richard Croaker, a part played by Errol Flynn in the stage production at the Royal Theatre, Northampton in 1933. Pat had been married less than a year when she started filming *The Farmer's Wife.* "Acting is satisfying a life-long urge, but I don't neglect my home. I'm a good wife," she told Norman Lee, the film's screenwriter and co-director. What a load of rubbish! Pat was flirtatious by nature, and when she met Wilding for the first time she was immediately drawn to his relaxed, easy-going style. It was a style that contrasted markedly with the rather staid husband she regretted marrying. She instantly fell 'head over heels' in love with Wilding and more than likely, the philandering Wilding with her. Wasting no time, on their first night together they went to Pat's dressing room, and within minutes were making love. It must have been an amazing site for Wilding, seeing a woman as beautiful as Pat lying naked on the bed, and crazy about him. This was the real Pat, a woman whose prim and virginal looks belied a woman whose passion easily matched Wilding's.

By now Hitler had started his bombing campaign on Britain, so, in order to protect the actors from London air-raids, and insure that none of the completed filming would have to be re-shot if any of them got injured during an enemy bombing attack, they all had to agree to live at the studio for the duration of the film, by turning their dressing rooms into 'bed-sits'. This cosy arrangement was perfect for Pat and Wilding to pursue their torrid affair.

As their passion for one another shone through on the screen, it is questionable whether Murray, who would often drive down to the studios at the weekend, was aware of the affair. But even if he didn't have his suspicions, Kay Young, Wilding's actress wife whom he married in 1937, almost certainly did. Throughout her career, Pat, like several movie stars – Jean Simmons was another - meticulously kept an autograph book, and would get the stars and crew with whom she worked to add their signature, and usually a short message. It was an album that she looked at from time to time in later years to remind her of the good times she had had whilst working in the film industry.

On the opposite page of the album autographed by Michael Wilding after he'd finished filming *The Farmer's Wife*, his wife sarcastically wrote:

'To my dear Bunny,
Not only do I have to face my husband every day of the week, I find I have to face him on the opposite page; it's not that I wish it – but Oh! I wish it were Murray 'sweet tobacco' Laing – I wonder why he always looks so humped up??? My love, Kay Wilding'

There is no doubt that Pat's intense relationship with Wilding hastened the collapse of Wilding's marriage to Kay, though it would be a further ten years before they divorced. If this troubled Pat, it didn't show. Throughout her life, wives posed no obstacle for her if she *fell in love*, as she so often did, with their husbands. In fact, her flagrant and somewhat scandalous affairs with married men earned her the name 'bedrock' within the film industry, a name she was familiar with, but did not question. It was one of her best friends, actress Christine Norden, not a shrinking violet herself, who claimed that Pat was astonishingly always eager for sex.

Born in Leigh-on-Sea on 23 July 1912, Michael Wilding became a commercial artist when he left school. In 1933 he joined the art department of a London film studio, where he was approached by producers to become a movie star-in-training due to his dashing good looks. He appeared in a number of films during the 1930s, most of them in uncredited roles, before gaining acceptance in more leading roles. It was thanks to the unavailability of Rex Harrison and John Mills, busy with other film commitments, that Wilding became a bit of a matinee idol in the late 1940s when Herbert Wilcox cast him with Anna Neagle in his 'London series'; *Piccadilly Incident, The Courtneys of Curzon Street, Spring in Park Lane* and *Maytime in Mayfair*. But it was for his much-publicised marriage to Elizabeth Taylor in February 1952 that Michael Wilding will probably be best remembered. Following their marriage, which only lasted five years, he went to Hollywood to try his luck as an actor, but Hedda Hopper, the acerbic showbiz columnist, more or less put paid to that when she said that he and Stewart Granger were more than just good friends. A $2million lawsuit followed, which Wilding won. He was in fact, anything but gay. The many women who came into contact with him - Anna Neagle, who like Pat fell hopelessly in love with him, Ingrid Bergman, Margaret Leighton and Marlene Dietrich, who was quite put out when he married Elizabeth Taylor instead of her, could all vouch for Wilding's masculinity. Little wonder that Pat fell for this man, who had all the endearing qualities that she longed for, but were in short supply when it came to Murray.

***

"The antidote for war time blues is laughter, and picture-goers will be infected with hilarity when they see *The Farmer's Wife*" was how ABPC announced the film when it was released in April 1941. But there were occasions when it was anything but 'laughter' when the film was being made. On one occasion during location filming of a fairground scene, a German aircraft, on its way to bomb nearby Luton, swooped down and sprayed the film crew and actors with machine gun bullets. "Fortunately," said Pat, "we all huddled in the hedge to avoid the bullets coming down and nobody was injured, but we did see the black mushroom of smoke where they had bombed a Luton factory." That day was Friday 30 August when twenty enemy bombers targeted Luton, killing 59 civilians and injuring almost two hundred others. "Pat didn't show any sign of fear," wrote Norman Lee in his book *Log of a Director*. "I hope they don't drop any big stuff that will ruin the day's work," Pat casually said to him.

On another occasion, a scene called for a bull to run amok amongst a crowd of extras across a fairground. "We hired a beast with enormous shoulders, short legs and wicked eyes which broke loose twice when we weren't ready for it," recalled Lee, adding; "I sought shelter under a van whilst Leslie Arliss took refuge on a roundabout."

This was the first film Leslie Arliss directed, which he did jointly with Norman Lee. It wasn't until he joined Gainsborough Pictures, where he directed some of the most flamboyant and successful films during World War Two, a couple of which starred Patricia Roc; *Love Story* and *The Wicked Lady*, that he was catapulted into the public eye.

During the film, Pat is supposed to sing *Love's Old Sweet Song*, but although she had a pleasant singing voice, Lee decided not to risk it and got seventeen-year-old Millicent Phillips, a popular radio singer at the time, to dub Pat's voice. For a long time afterwards, according to Pat, she was getting numerous offers to sing at concerts.

The Farmer's Wife had a strong cast, which included Wilfrid Lawson and Nora Swinburne, whom Pat described as 'an absolute sweetheart'. But the strangest casting was that of twenty-year-old Welsh actor Kenneth Griffith who was supposed to be Pat's boyfriend in the picture, before she swapped him for Michael Wilding's character. Griffith's inclusion was mainly due to the lack of young actors, who by now were serving in the armed forces. Film companies had to make do with whoever was available at the time. Often, the small pool of actors that producers could call on were like Griffith, servicemen who been invalided out of military service for one reason or another. In Griffith's case, he volunteered for the RAF in 1939 but was later released because of poor health. Stewart Granger, who made a name for himself during the war, was another actor invalided out of the army. He suffered from a serious stomach ulcer, a condition that was to dog him throughout his life. Then there were the conscientious objectors such as Pat's friend, James Mason, who refused to take up arms on the grounds that he was a pacifist. Noël Coward, in a patriotic gesture, refused to cast Mason in his wartime film *In Which We Serve*.

With *The Farmer's Wife* completed, it wasn't long before Pat was back at the Welwyn studios for her second film under an ABPC two picture deal secured by her agent Eric Goodhead. The film was *My Wife's Family*, an archetypal British farce about a number of misunderstandings within a family. "Altogether rather silly and the direction, in the hands of Walter Mycroft, unimaginative," was the verdict of the *Monthly Film Bulletin.* At the time, Pat was still heavily involved with Michael Wilding who, quite fortuitously, was filming *Spring Meeting* at the same studios. "I absolutely adored Michael," Pat admitted to Henry Jaremko when he interviewed her in 2000, as she recalled the evening he and eight others, including Noël Coward, played strip poker at her Eaton House flat. She didn't say whether her much cheated-on husband was at this party, but in any case, the marriage was all but over, even though they remained living together as man and wife for a while longer.

"Like so many wartime marriages, it just didn't work out. Apart from our age difference, I wanted to start a family and Murray didn't, and eventually we just drifted apart," explained Pat years later. This seemed a rather convenient and tidy way of dismissing the marriage, which was, without doubt, an utter disaster from the start.

Yet again, the cast of *My Wife's Family* had to live at the studio for the duration of the film, which suited most of the cast, especially Chili Bouchier, who played Rosa, a young flirty actress, in the picture. "Personally I found it sheer heaven to be able to tumble out of bed straight into the make-up room without a long journey at the crack of dawn," she recalled in her autobiography, *Shooting Star: the last of the silent film stars.*

Regarded as the British cinema's first female sex symbol, Chili Bouchier and Pat became very good friends, a friendship which continued over the years. In 1996, when the BBC's 'victim' in their *This is Your Life* series was Chili Bouchier, one of her surprise guests was Pat, now eighty, who willingly flew over from her home in Switzerland to take part in the show. Introduced by Michael Aspel as "one of the great stars from the golden age of cinema", this was Pat's last professional appearance of any kind.

The complimentary remarks Pat bestowed on Miss Bouchier, concluding with, "It has been a lovely privilege to take part in your tribute," revealed nothing of the dramas of their early days as friends, when Chili became Pat's confidante. There were many an occasions when she had to cover for Pat during the latter's clandestine meetings with Wilding, when her chronic and obsessively jealous husband Murray was on the prowl looking for her. The strain of all this took its toll on Pat. She began to drink quite heavily, a problem which plagued her for the rest of her life, and on several occasions she would drink far more than was good for her. Talking with Michael Thornton, Chili Bouchier recalled one hair-raising lunch with Pat. "Pat, who was dodging telephone calls from her suspicious and furious husband, had drunk far too much and was being violently sick in the ladies. She asked me to fabricate some cock and bull story about her whereabouts when he phoned again, and quite naturally I obliged," said, a lady who was not exactly a stranger to sexual intrigue.

Pat's affair with Michael Wilding eventually came to an end. "He was probably the love of my life. I would have married him in a second if we'd both been free," Pat has since admitted. "But sadly there was nothing to be done about it. Michael was married at the time and I was of course married. It was a mess." They did, however, remain very good friends up until Wilding's premature death in 1979 following a fall down a long flight of stairs during an epileptic seizure. He was a few days short of his sixty-seventh birthday. In his autobiography *Michael Wilding – Apple Sauce – the story of my life* published three years after his death, he does not mention Patricia Roc. It is an amusing, breezy book that reflects his good humour rather than the gruelling details of his private life.

***

Pat managed to keep busy making films throughout the war years, but there were some that she would have loved to have been in, but missed out for one reason or another. For instance, she had a cruel disappointment when she lost out to Deborah Kerr, the part of the tragic heroine, Mary Brodie, in the film adaptation of A. J. Cronin's novel, *Hatter's Castle.* Margaret Lockwood was originally going to play the role, but before shooting got under way she announced that she was pregnant and had to drop out. Pat was anxious to replace her, and with a little inside help from James Mason, one of her close friends, thought that she had won the part. "It was a film I would love to have made, but Deborah Kerr got it instead of me, and I might add, played it very badly," said a slightly embittered Pat. Had she landed the part of Mary Brodie, and played it with the same convictions as Miss Kerr, who deservedly received excellent reviews, Pat's film career may well have taken that giant leap forward she was looking for. As it was, she had to continue making lack lustre films, whilst doing her best to get away from the British studios' tendency of making their actresses nothing more than characterless ornaments.

Nevertheless, Pat was steadily getting noticed by the cinema going public, and was beginning to acquire a growing number of British fans. In June 1941, one such fan, Brian Houghton from Hornchurch, wrote to *Picturegoer* in response to Malcolm Phillips' article 'Starlets', in which he asserted that the only starlets of note were American. An indignant Houghton responded in his letter to the editor, saying: "Phillips does not know what he is talking about. One British starlet worth watching is certainly Patricia Roc."

Michael Hodgson

CHAPTER FIVE

'Sexy bouncy girl next door'

PAT'S next picture looked more promising than it really was. In *Let the People Sing*, she teamed up with Alastair Sim, Fred Emney and Oliver Wakefield in John Baxter's adaptation of a J. B. Priestley novel in which he expressed the morals concerning the virtues of democracy and the importance of public alertness. The film, which Baxter also produced and directed, was made at the large Rock Studios at Elstree for British National. It was only mildly popular at the box office and the critics of the day hated it. William Whitebait in the *New Statesman* for instance, complained:

'The dialogue is flat; the photography dull to the point of ugliness; and the whole thing shows that ingenious, happy-go-lucky mediocrity which used to be the glum hallmark of English films.'

Fourth billed as Hope Ollerton, Pat added glamour to the role of 'a girl of the people', whose spirit captivates Sir Reginald Foxfield (Oliver Wakefield). In the film she schemes to save a town's music hall from being taken over, both by museum-loving dullards, and a group of commercial profiteers. Pat gets plenty of coverage and sings twice in the film, but it really was a vehicle for the old timers; music hall comedian Edward Rigby, and Fred Emney who stole every scene he was in. When *Variety* reviewed the film, in which Peter Ustinov played an uncredited cameo role, it thought that it was, 'Mainly word painting minus dramatic action, with relatively little opportunity for the comparatively few feminine roles.' The film may well have been a bit of a let down at the time, but today, imperfections in technique seem less important than the film's enthusiasm for life well away from London's Mayfair.

As usual, Pat asked those associated with the film to add their autograph to her book, which they did, with the exception of one of the actors, Alastair Sim.

He was notorious for never signing autographs, not because he thought it was beneath him, but beneath the would-be autograph hunter. Could Sim really have considered Pat, one of the nicest stars of her day, to be in that category – well, he didn't sign her book!

In February 1942, Pat began shooting her third film at the Welwyn Studios, a thriller-come-gangster story with the title, *Suspected Person*. It was, by British standards, quite a good picture at the time and gave Pat a chance to shine in one of her first major roles. Her co-star and brother in the plot was the Welsh actor, Clifford Evans. He played Jim Raynor who, whilst in America, gets mixed up with a pair of bank robbers Franklin and Dolan played by Robert Beatty and Eric Clavering. When Franklin and Dolan follow Raynor to England because they think he has doubled- crossed them and run of with the proceeds from the robbery, Inspector Thompson (David Farrar) of Scotland Yard gets involved. "One of the best made thrillers of late in which Patricia Roc gives an adequate performance as Joan," wrote the critic for the *Monthly Film Bulletin*.

Written and ably directed by Lawrence Huntington, the story calls for a lot of the action to take place at Euston railway station in London, which Huntington 'reconstructed' at the Welwyn studios. Even though it was one of the most expensive sets to have been built at the time, apparently it was cheaper than location filming, and besides, the capital was still subject to Hitler's bombing raids and Huntington didn't want to risk actors and crew in London.

In the summer of 1942, Pat was at the Riverside Studios in Hammersmith to begin work on little more than an unassuming star vehicle for the 'forces sweetheart', Vera Lynn. When shooting began on 1 June 1942, the film had the title *Sincerely Yours,* but was later changed to *We'll Meet Again*, the song title of Vera Lynn's greatest hit. Released in November, *We'll Meet Again* became one of the most successful British pictures at the box-office in 1943. It attracted massive audiences, many of them men serving in the armed forces, who went to see their idol Vera Lynn, but found themselves in the presence of the lovely Patricia Roc.

Twenty-five year old Miss Lynn was angular of features, and the camera was not always kind to her, so the film image, to the eyes of the servicemen did not match the golden voice they were accustomed to hearing over the radio. Instead, they focused on Patricia Roc. "My fan mail shot up following that film, especially from the service men," she said. "In one letter, one wag even suggested that I was now 'the forces sweetheart', but I couldn't sing and Vera could," she added. Few would disagree that Pat was one of Britain's most attractive stars of her era. Aware of her own star image, she summed up her own particular appeal as: "the bouncy, sexy girl next door that mothers would like their sons to have married – and the sons wouldn't have minded either." How right she was!

In *We'll Meet Again*, Lynn plays the part of Peggy Brown, a natural born singer who has a crush on Bruce MacIntosh, played by Donald Gray. But he, like the servicemen, only has eyes for Peggy's best friend, Ruth, Pat's character. Through the most trying of circumstances, Peggy remains good friends with both, as she discovers meaning in her singing career, entertaining the troops and generally boosting morale throughout the country.

South African Donald Gray was a Captain in The King's Own Scottish Borderers and had been granted special leave from his army duties to make *We'll Meet Again*. After the war he continued his acting career, even though he had lost his left arm in July 1944 at Caen, to a German anti-tank shell. He is best remembered today for his portrayal as one-armed detective Mark Saber in the television series of the same name that ran from 1956 to 1962.

As for Dame Vera Lynn, (she was created a Dame Commander of the Order of the British Empire in 1975) she has become legendary, not just in the United Kingdom, but throughout the world, for her singing and charitable work. But it seems that she was not that enamoured with the film industry. In her autobiography *Vocal Refrain*, she devoted just one page to her 'film career' - she made two other films besides *We'll Meet Again*; *Rhythm Serenade* in 1943 and *One Exciting Night* in 1944 – and appeared to have been extremely bored with the whole set-up, especially when making *We'll Meet Again*. "It was the hanging about, rather than filming, which was so tiring," she wrote.

Conversely, Patricia Roc, who loved making films, usually stayed on the movie set whether she was needed or not, to observe the action in order to maintain the tempo of the story line. "Working on that film with Vera Lynn was a lot of fun," said Pat, something that Dame Vera could not remember. "Unfortunately," she said, I did not really see a lot of Pat off set. Although we worked together, we didn't really get together afterwards."

Pat was at last in a picture that was a huge box-office success, and even though her part was not as built up as Vera Lynn's, it did her no harm at all. Stardom was just around the corner.

Pat with thirteen-year-old Peggy Cummins having some fun whilst making 'Dr 'Dowd (Author's Private Collection)

Pat as a reluctant smoker
A scene from 'Pack Up Your Troubles'
(Author's Private Collection)

Pat and Michael Wilding togerther in
'The Farmer's Wife'
(Author's Private Collection)

Pat remained friends with Kay Wilding.
Here they are arriving fort the London
Premier of David Leans 'Oliver Twist' on 28 June
1948 (Authors Private Collection)

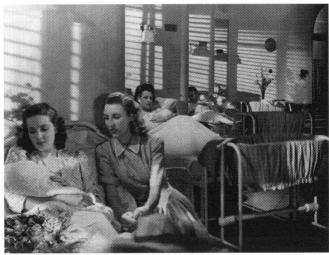

Pat visited in the maternity ward by Vera Lynn – a scene from 'We'll Meet Again'
(Courtesy of Brian Twist)

CHAPTER SIX

One of the Gainsborough Girls

CAROLINE Lejeune, in her review for *The Observer*, said of *Millions Like Us*: "If there were no other reason than its delicate, shy love story, tenderly played by Patricia Roc and Gordon Jackson, *Millions Like Us* should be sure of a warm welcome". The London's *Evening Standard* raved: "Patricia Roc plays the part with great delicacy and force". The film, considered to be one of Patricia Roc's greatest achievements, marked the beginning of a transitional period in her career. Film historians insist she never did better work. Robert Murphy called her performance 'charismatic'.

Against stiff competition, Pat passed her audition with flying colours and Ted Black offered her the leading role in the film. Playing Celia Crowson, the reserved younger daughter of a war-torn working class family, was without doubt a defining moment in the film career of Patricia Roc. This was her big chance and she wasn't about to let it slip. After shooting a few scenes, Black and Maurice Ostrer, the powerful and much feared head of Gainsborough Pictures, studied her on film and liked what they saw. Always on the lookout for bright young actresses who knew how to put in a good performance, Ostrer offered Pat an exclusive seven-year contract. When Eric, her agent, explained the financial terms, Pat almost did cartwheels around his office. She would receive £1050, which was worth about £38,600 in 2013 - *in the rest of this book approximate equivalent 2013 currency values will be shown in square brackets, thus [£38,600]* - for 30 days work, plus £35 [£1,290] a day for any additional work she did during the first year, rising to £1,350 [£49,800] plus £45 [£1,650] a day in the second year. It was quite a fortune in those days if you consider that the average price of a house was £500 [£18,500]. It was also important in those days to have a studio behind you, somebody to present you properly, to groom and develop you - as Gainsborough had done for Margaret Lockwood ever since she had become a contract player in 1937.

Exchanging freedom for security, on 24 February 1943, over a 6d. postage stamp, Pat quite happily signed away seven years of her life to the prodigious production company, even though it meant that Gainsborough, which in effect now belonged to the Rank Organisation, would in future be able to choose her film roles, and to a certain extent control her life. It also meant that the Gainsborough's publicity machine and planned programme of films, in which the same group of contract artists appeared in 'picture after picture', would ensure that she was always in the public eye. As her friend and now Gainsborough colleague James Mason once said, "a star who is not constantly thrusting his face at the public, very soon finds he is no longer in demand."

Pat's contract stipulated that she must comply with all reasonable requirements, directions and requests, including the studio's decision to loan her out to another studio if necessary, send her up and down the country on publicity tours, and appear in advertisements for products such as Lux toilet soap, Drene shampoo and Miner's cosmetics. She was also encouraged, as were all the stars, to wear clothes designed by well-known fashion houses. According to Black, off screen behaviour was as important to the fans as actual film roles themselves. "The public," he said, "expected glamour from their favourites." For Margaret Lockwood this was a bit of a problem who, on one occasion, turned up at an important film premiere in a raincoat and beret. It was quite the opposite for Pat; she always looked immaculate, whether turning up at the studio early in the morning, or going out in the evening.

Millions Like Us was an important film, not just for Pat but for the government too. With the working title 'Women Without Uniforms', the film was commissioned by the Ministry of Information (MoI), who, summarised by Sue Harper in her book *Women in British Cinema*, 'was anxious to address a female problem: the low levels of recruitment and poor morale of women in factory work during the war'. The MoI hired Sidney Gilliat and Frank Launder to write the script, something they did for half their normal fee to 'help the war effort', and persuaded Gainsborough to make the film. Ted Black, striving to break new ground by making populist realism films at Gainsborough, was more than happy to take it on, unlike Maurice Ostrer, who thought the whole project ludicrous. He was convinced that film-goers were tiring of war themes and were ready for escapist pictures to help take their minds off the realities outside the cinema for a couple of hours. Instead, he busied himself with the first of a highly successful series of costume melodramas, *The Man in Grey*, with Margaret Lockwood, James Mason, Phyllis Calvert and newcomer Stewart

Granger. It was in this series of Ostrer's bodice-rippers that Pat would eventually feature.

The story of *Millions Like Us* at first concentrates on the members of the Crowson family, and in particular Celia, one of two daughters who receives her call-up papers following the outbreak of the war. Her vision of chauffeuring Generals or nursing wounded heroes are dashed when she is sent to Birmingham to work in the huge aircraft factory at Castle Bromwich, (which the Luftwaffe bombed not long after the film units had left) and billeted in a hostel along with many other female conscripts. There, Celia meets and marries Fred Blake (Gordon Jackson) a young airman in the R.A.F., who is later killed during a bombing raid over Germany.

Even though the *Sunday Times* film critic thought: 'Miss Roc a trifle ritzy for the part', Celia in fact is a deliberately ordinary heroine, shy and unglamorous. It is arguably one of Pat's best and only thoroughly satisfying performances, encouraged as she was by Gilliat and Launder to under-act and restrain the exuberant energy which tended to spoil many of her previous and, come to that, some of her later performances. The love scene between Pat and Gordon Jackson, filmed by ace cameraman Jack Cox, showing two inarticulate working-class characters attempting to express their feelings for each other, was ground-breaking simply because it was so unfussily handled by Gilliat and Launder. "I don't suppose you'd like to marry me?" Fred asks Celia in a crowded pub. "I don't mind," she replies.

Ealing Studios loaned Gordon Jackson out to Gainsborough on the understanding that he shared top billing with Pat. It was only his third film and still nineteen, eight years younger than Pat, which might explain why Gilliat and Launder were a bit worried about the love scenes between him and Pat. "They said I always held Pat as if she were a time bomb," said Jackson. "Oh, that darling, darling man – he was so sweet, just lovely," said Pat about Jackson in 1990 when she heard that he had died. Today, he is probably best remembered for his role as Hudson, the austere butler in the popular London Weekend Television's series *Upstairs, Downstairs*, which ran from 1971 to 1975.

***

The strengths of *Millions Like Us* lie in the unswerving devotion to reality, clever dialogue and its cast, which included Megs Jenkins, Anne Crawford, Moore Marriott and the somewhat difficult Eric Portman. He didn't want to play the part of a factory foreman and went up to Halifax and got drunk but, threatened with suspension by Ted Black, he made the film and turned in a good performance. Then of course there was Patricia Roc, who acted with sincerity throughout. With her hair scraped back and wearing plain frocks, she stepped straight from the screen into the hearts of the public with her gentle ways and simple emotional acting. The volume of fan mail she received after the film was released in October 1943 was staggering. Letters flooded in, not just from the male population, but women too, who found her honest and daring portrayal of the modern young woman refreshing. *Picturegoer,* the most widely read British film fan magazine at the time, celebrated Pat's sincerity in an article in which the writer stated that:

> "In everything she does, Patricia Roc is sincere and genuine. She hates pretence and posing, which accounts for her enormous popularity in the studio and with the public."

For Pat, working at Gainsborough was a dream come true. She had security, and following the rave notices of *Millions Like Us*, she just knew that she was going to be a successful film star. But fitting in at Gainsborough with the other contract players, Phyllis Calvert and Margaret Lockwood in particular, wasn't as straightforward as it might have seemed. There was a pecking order at the studios, one that was jealously guarded by the established stars. Phyllis Calvert once said: "Working at Gainsborough was a little club. Patricia Roc and Jean Kent came later, so they weren't given the leading parts until they sort of waited – that was the technique of the studio, that you started with small parts and worked up to big parts." Jean Kent was a little more forthcoming with her memories of how it worked; "First Margaret Lockwood, then Pat Roc and Phyllis Calvert, then me. I was the odds-and-sods girl who would get the parts that the others didn't want to do."

Pat's next film, *2000 Women*, a drama set in a women's internment camp in Nazi-occupied France, put this theory to the test. Phyllis Calvert decided that she didn't want to play the part of Rosemary Brown, a novice nun, who falls in love with a British airman hiding from the Germans, even though the part had been specially written for her by Frank Launder and Sidney Gilliat. According to Calvert, *falling in love* was unlikely behaviour for any nun with even the slightest vocation. Launder, who directed the film, gave the part to Pat, now one of the 'Gainsborough girls'. She accepted it with open arms, and made a far more convincing nun than Calvert could ever have done. Calvert played the tough talking journalist Freda Thompson, although this didn't suit the temperamental star either. She wanted to swap roles with Jean Kent, who had been cast as a prostitute in the film, but Launder would not allow Calvert to get the better of him a second time.

Apart from Pat, Phyllis Calvert and Jean Kent, there were several other familiar faces, each playing an essential role in the story, faces such as Anne Crawford, Flora Robson, Muriel Aked, Thora Hird, Reneé Houston, Dulcie Gray, and Betty Jardine who sadly died the following year during childbirth. Each put in a reliable performance, making it difficult to single out anyone who out-shone the other. As for Pat, still under the influence of Frank Launder's direction, she gave a nuanced performance as the nun who is hiding the secret that she was, before the war, a music hall performer called Mary Maugham.

Launder, who culled the material for *2000 Women* from two showgirls who had escaped from a women's internment camp at Vittel in France, explores how women fare under pressure. Their camaraderie and resilience takes many forms: a bath becomes a lively social event, they organise classes and concerts, and even break out in spontaneous defiance, applauding when Frau Holweg (Christina Forbes) announces that three British airmen, who have bailed out of their stricken bomber, have infiltrated the building. It also flirts around the issue of lesbianism. When Phyllis Calvert first sees Teresa (Betty Jardine) the butch 'head girl' figure, she says, "To think I used to have a crush on a girl like that at school". Miss Manningford (Flora Robson) and Miss Meredith (Muriel Aked) are certainly closer to the subject of lesbianism than the censor would have wanted depicted. Flora Robson has a wonderful scene when she persuades a German officer to let her share a room with her companion. Muriel Aked who, when told that she will have to share with Flora Robson, has for a split second a half-hidden look of absolute glee.

What would Alfred Hitchcock have made of the film? It was offered to him by Launder who thought it was just right for him. "I cabled Hitchcock with a brief outline of the story and he promptly replied, offering to buy it. But after discussing the idea with producer Ted Black, he encouraged me to make it myself," explained Launder.

When *2000 Women* was released on 6 November 1944, it was a huge commercial success. However, the predominantly male critical establishment was sniffy and dismissive; 'Trivial and silly' said *The Listener* about the film, but Pat got her usual compliments about her looks: 'Patricia Roc is a very beautiful and appealing Rosemary' said *Kinematograph Weekly*. When the American cinemagoers saw the film they could be forgiven if they were a trifle baffled by the plot. The American distributor for some quirky reason retitled the film *House of 1000 Women* - perhaps they did a head count - and cut it from 93 minutes to 60, and ignored Pat's adventures as a nun completely.

Now financially secure, Pat had finally walked out on Murray for good. She had come to realise all too quickly that he was not a man she could love. He stayed in the Mayfair flat whilst she took a smart flat at 49 Hallam Street, just around the corner from the BBC's headquarters in Upper Regent Street. But the split didn't stop the jealous husband from spying on her. He would often call at the Islington studio when Pat was filming scenes for *2000 Women*, on the pretence of seeing her to discuss the terms of their separation. Whenever he did, and 'bedroc' was *entertaining* a man in her dressing room, word had to get to her quickly that Murray Laing was on the prowl. It was episodes such as these that didn't go unnoticed by Phyllis Calvert. In Pat's autograph book she wrote: "Here's hoping that the 'penitent Nun' will have a new meaning for you in the future!"

When Pat moved into her flat, she immediately injected her own feminine personality into it, re-decorating it in a colour scheme of soft green with touches of wine throughout, and furnishing it with Queen Anne style furniture, wine coloured carpets and damask curtains and upholstery in a soft eau de nil. She felt comfortable and safe there; able to live the life she had dreamt of for quite some time. Whilst she was more than capable of looking after the one-bedroom flat herself, Pat decided she needed help. She employed Pauline Fletcher, a lady who travelled from Clapham daily to Hallam Street, as her maid and confidante. In one of her 1947 fan magazines, about Pauline, Pat wrote:

> Pauline really spoils me. When I'm busy at the studio she is ironing my clothes, getting the shopping, doing all the chores at home and, even though I am a very good cook, she prepares my evening meal for me. Oh yes, she looks after my 'best friend' Breezy, a black and white cocker spaniel and my two adorable love birds when I am not at home. What would I do without her!

It was while Pat was living in the Hallam Street flat (which, according to Matthew Sweet in his book *Shepperton Babylon*, she shared with a prosperous prostitute – which was most unlikely) that two long-time residents in the same block of flats remembered Pat having a compromising encounter with David Niven during an air-raid. At that time, Niven was staying at the Ritz Hotel where he was writing the script, with Peter Ustinov and Eric Ambler, for a moral boosting film about the army called *The Way Ahead.*

Pat had known Niven for some time, and their amorous adventure that evening probably wasn't their first. When he was making *The First of the Few* in 1942 he tried very hard to convince Leslie Howard, who directed and starred in the film, that Pat was 'just right' for the lead female role, but Howard wasn't impressed. He considered her to be a tad too glamorous, and cast Rosamund John instead. Reminiscing with film historian Brian McFarlane, Miss John recalled:

> "I was up a tree at Robert Donat's house, picking cherries, when a girl I knew in an agency telephoned to say that Leslie Howard was looking for someone for his new film about the Air-Force. She suggested me and I had to go straight away. Leslie said I didn't look like an actress and decided to test me for the part of the wife...and I got it. I got on very well with him and luckily he didn't want to get me into bed, as he did with quite a few people he worked with."

Keeping his trousers on, and his hands firmly in his pockets was no doubt something to do with the fact that Rosamund John was heavily involved with Robert Donat at the time, and Howard didn't want to upset a fellow actor. Donat was a very big star with a lot of influence in those days, having starred in several important films including Hitchcock's classic thriller *Thirty Nine Steps,* and MGM's version of *Goodbye Mr. Chips,* for which he won the Oscar for best actor in 1939.

Pat and Rosamund John co-starred together a few years later in Gainsborough's *When the Bough Breaks.* "We joked about the casting of *The First of the Few* when we met up and how I narrowly missed ending up in Leslie Howard's bed," joked Pat. In fact, Howard would probably have had better luck with Pat when employing his seductive prowess, had he put her in his film instead of Rosamund John.

No sooner had Pat finished filming *2000 Women,* than she was off to Cornwall to star in the lachrymose *Love Story.* Her co-stars were Stewart Granger and Margaret Lockwood, an actress who had the reputation of being a no nonsense woman, and very protective of her star image. It was said that 'she liked to rule the roost', and there were several actresses who did not like working with her for that very reason. Jean Kent was one, whilst Kathleen Byron, who starred with Lockwood in *Madness of the Heart* in 1949, disliked her intensely. Speculation had it that Pat and Lockwood might clash when they were paired together. This however proved unfounded, especially as Pat's part required her to wear unglamorous dungarees and a head scarf for many of her scenes, which no doubt appeased *La Lockwood* to some extent.

Playing rivals in love for the affections of Stewart Granger, each was required to slap the other around the face. Recalled Pat; "I didn't pull my punches but neither did Maggie. In my autograph book, she wrote"

'*Love Story* is the first picture we have made together and I have to sock you on the jaw, not once but twice – here's hoping that in our next we can be friends, not enemies.' "

That wasn't to be when more 'jaw socking' occurred in their next picture together. It wasn't long, and not surprising, before rumours started circulating that the two *divas* hated one another. That, in fact couldn't have been further from the truth. Away from the studio they were the best of friends. "I have always been very close to both Maggie and Phyl (Phyllis Calvert) and working with them was a joy. I was particularly close to Maggie and we were very, very good friends. Sadly, she died a lonely woman," recalled Pat, adding, "There was never any vanity or rivalry, we were the Gainsborough girls."

Stewart Granger, in his autobiography *Sparks Fly Upward*, described *Love Story* as 'the biggest load of crap I'd ever read'. He wasn't far wrong; the plot lacks plausibility. The story revolves around a series of incredible misunderstandings and misplaced loyalties. Lissa, Margaret Lockwood's character, is a successful concert pianist who, learning that she has a serious heart condition and only a year to live, retreats to Cornwall where she falls in love with Kit, played by Granger. He is an R.A.F. pilot who sustained an injury whilst on active service, resulting in him going blind. Neither of them knows about each other's problems or that Judy, Pat's character, a chain-smoking theatre director and Kit's childhood sweetheart, is secretly in love with him. The two women fight over Kit like a couple of dogs over a bone. The love triangle is finally resolved when Kit proposes to Judy. Ripping a cigarette from her mouth as she saws at a loaf of bread, she declines Kit's proposal and relinquishes him to Lissa, knowing that it is on a temporary basis.

Needless to say, the critics had a field day: "It's simpering, it's mawkish, it makes one squirm in one's fauteuil. Why, I ask piteously, did Gainsborough Pictures choose to make it?" wrote the critic for *Time and Tide*. The British cinemagoers didn't agree. In just twelve weeks, *Love Story* took £200,000 [£7,300,000] at the box office, making it the second most profitable British film of the war years, because, for all its hyped emotions, the film is solidly rooted in wartime Britain and struck a chord with many of those who saw it.

"We're all living dangerously," Granger tells Lockwood. "There isn't any certainty any more…let's take the happiness we can, while we can," he says, echoing Pat's own sentiment five years earlier when she married Murray Laing.

The film was directed and co-written by Leslie Arliss, who believed in sacrificing action for emotion. He claimed that British films and British players were afraid of genuine emotion on the screen, and maintained that this was the reason for the supremacy of the Americans in human dramas.

In *Love Story*, Pat was the 'bad girl' who loved a man so intensely that she would stoop to deceit and lies to keep him for herself. Arliss encouraged her to show the right amount of ruthlessness as Judy, whose tough exterior masks her overwhelming love for the unsuspecting Kit. Explained Arliss, "This character intrigued me, I felt that so many women in real life would have acted in the same way. Self-sacrifice may be very beautiful, but it is the exception rather than the rule in real life." In a letter from Leslie Arliss to Pat, he wrote:

"The part of Judy comes out just as I imagined it in my most hopeful daydreams – and I'm sure you'll be as happy as I am about it."

Today's Cinema was in agreement, saying: "Patricia Roc once again demonstrates that she is an actress of no mean talent in the ungrateful role of Judy made selfish by love."

Up until now Patricia Roc had been destined to play the beautiful young ingénue, usually 'sweet and sincere', so the part of Judy was a new departure for her, and she played it convincingly. In a railway farewell scene with Stewart Granger, who is going away to hospital for what may be a fatal operation in an attempt to cure his blindness, Pat acts realistically. Watching him kiss Margaret Lockwood goodbye is unbearable for her. Finally, when he dismisses Pat's character with a light thank you, she is overcome by her emotions and kisses him passionately, unable to contain her hidden love for him any longer. This scene contains some of the best acting in British films of that period and it was noted that Margaret Lockwood congratulated Pat, even though it was thought by many that Pat had stolen the film from Lockwood. In fact, the producers cut a later scene when it was thought that Pat was winning sympathy away from the 'star'. But no matter how good Pat was in the film – and in *Love Story* she was very good – this was always meant to be a Margaret Lockwood picture and she ultimately got the plaudits from the critics.

When the film premiered in October, Pat was busy in Cornwall making *Johnny Frenchman* for Michael Balcon. Leslie Arliss desperately wanted her to be in attendance. He wrote saying:

> 'The premiere of *Love Story* is at the Gaumont, Haymarket on Monday evening, 9 October. I am most anxious for you to be there so that you can reap some of the rewards for your really lovely work in the film. They are putting on a 100 per cent *Love Story* broadcast programme in 'Music From the Movies' on the previous Saturday night, October 7 … dollops of music, and then one or two high spot scenes between you and Margaret.
>
> Do you think you'll be able to come up for it? It is really terribly important – the broadcast will help the premiere and the film no end – and I've written to Micky Balcon begging him to try very hard to let you have those few days off. Do please do everything you can, Pat, to get up – at any rate for the broadcast. If you can stay on for the premiere, we're having a party at the Savoy afterwards and would love you to come. Please see what you can do.
>
> Goodbye, Pat, and do your damnedest to get up for the seventh.
>
> Love, Leslie'

Michael Balcon agreed that Pat should be present at both the broadcast and the premiere and gave her the necessary time off which enabled her to go to the Savoy dinner too. But missing from that dinner was Stewart Granger. He threw a 'hissy' and declined Arliss's invitation, because, in one scene in the film, Granger was asked to dive from a Cornish cliff into the sea. Granger refused to do it and said his stand-in should do it in long shot. For whatever reason, Arliss chose a bowlegged short stand-in to make the dive into the sea, which infuriated Granger. Arliss reputedly commented that Granger's absence from the dinner was his revenge for using an unflattering double.

Margaret Lockwood once described filming in the 1940s as representing a treadmill; 'going straight out of one picture into the next and doing as you were told'. Phyllis Calvert suggested it was more like 'being on a conveyor belt', as Pat was soon to find out. Almost before she had completed her scenes and removed the make-up she wore in *Love Story*, than she was back at the Riverside Studios to start work on her next film, Gainsborough's flamboyant extravaganza, *Madonna of the Seven Moons* with Phyllis Calvert and a second stint with Stewart Granger.

In the mid-1940s Gainsborough Pictures were making on average half a dozen pictures a year. Almost all of them were historical costume melodramas that were unique and different in style to any other of their British rivals. Moreover, the new genre provided the perfect showcase for the studio's stable of stars. Stars, like Patricia Roc, Margaret Lockwood, Phyllis Calvert, James Mason and Stewart Granger were all important to these pictures, larger than life icons to undergo larger than life trials and tribulations. Pat fitted in well with this regime, playing torrid, emotional roles that couldn't fail to make an impression on the audience. She was now a household name and one of Britain's top stars and she loved it. "I liked the atmosphere and I enjoyed everybody I worked with, although I know some of the actors weren't too keen on the roles they were asked to play. Jimmy (Stewart Granger) and James (Mason) ridiculed most of the films they did at Gainsborough and they finished up going to Hollywood. Phyl (Calvert) wasn't too keen either, but as far as I was concerned, for me each picture in those days was a new adventure," said Pat in later life.

Granger summed up his feelings when he was quoted as saying; "All my serious theatre training wasted on having to play these ridiculous and totally unreal characters in this kind of junk." Mason just thought they were "bloody codswallop"!

As with most of Gainsborough's films during that period, the critics panned *Madonna of the Seven Moons* when it was released in December 1944. The *New Statesman* thought it was 'notably bad, and that everything in the film was treacly - characters, dialogue, and situations'. The *Monthly Film Bulletin* commented on the 'the crude melodramatics of the story'. When the film was shown at the National Film Theatre in London in June 2003 however, the programme note indicated otherwise. "While the psychology is dubious, the excellent script raises the film above cliché and Phyllis Calvert expertly negotiates the dual role."

Based on a story by journalist and confirmed spiritualist Margery Lawrence, Pat plays the part of Angela, the nineteen-year-old daughter of Maddalena, a beautiful Italian woman with a split personality, played by Phyllis Calvert. The casting was bizarre if not downright silly because Pat was almost twenty-nine when the film was made and only three months younger than Calvert playing her mother.

The story revolves around Maddalena, a repressed, saintly, do-gooding banker's wife with no real life or mind of her own. But from time to time she vanishes to take up another existence as a sensuous, wanton gangster's moll called Rosanna, the plaything of swarthy, virile, knife-wielding Nino. A very reluctant Stewart Granger plays Nino, who engages in some uninhibited lovemaking with Calvert in scenes unusually explicit for the mid-1940s.

Angela, unlike her straight-laced mother, represents healthy modern womanhood, and acts with an easy unpuritanical manner. She smokes, drinks and much to her mother's disapproval, wears shorts. But Pat's wardrobe, designed by Elizabeth Haffenden, did not reflect the time when the action occurs (the thirties) but instead was pure mid-1940s. Following the trend of the American cinema, Gainsborough decided to updated the clothes (plus hairdos and makeup) from past decades, probably with an eye on female cinemagoers seeking the latest fashions.

Madonna of the Seven Moons was not one of Pat's favourite films. She, like many, thought it was one of the most bizarre of all of Gainsborough's costume melodramas, in which the 'Italian' characters talk and behave as though they've just stepped out of a Noël Coward play set in the Home Counties.

The tale is told in leisurely manner, with the director, Arthur Crabtree, dwelling overlong on characterising the heroine's idyllic domesticity in Florence, and the flirtatiousness, overt sexuality and independence of her daughter. But in spite of its faults and the critics' condemnation - "Novelettish balderdash killed stone dead by stilted presentation," was the opinion of critic Leslie Halliwell - the wartime cinemagoers flocked in their thousands to see the film. Costing £125,000 [£4.500,000} to make, much of this being spent on the sets described by Helen Fletcher in *Time and Tide* as 'some of the ugliest and most expensive ever contrived', it was a huge hit at the box-office and grossed £320,000 [£11,600,000] in just a few weeks, making it one of the most successful of Gainsborough's potboilers.

On 6 June 1944 the Allied forces began the invasion of Normandy. Pat remembered it well. "We were all feeling quite relieved that we only had a few more days filming to finish *Madonna* when the D-day landings were announced over the radio," she recalled. "I think the whole crew stopped work that day. We just huddled around the radio to find out what was happening.

We knew that victory was in sight, it was so exciting, but sad in many respects because we knew that there would be heavy casualties," she added.

Almost five years had passed since the outbreak of war, when Pat was contemplating her film career. Since then she had risen from an almost unknown to become one of Britain's leading ladies of the silver screen – and she was enjoying every minute of being a film star. Her adoring fans idolised her wherever she went. But it never occurred to her, or if it did, it didn't seem to worry her very much, that her personal life had become as different as it could be from the squeaky clean image she portrayed on the cinema screen. Oblivious or not to the studio gossip, Pat was about to steal another husband's affections from his wife, when she travelled to Cornwall to make her next picture.

Michael Balcon had been monitoring Pat's progress ever since he had cast her in *The Gaunt Stranger* six years previously. When he was putting together a cast for his new film, *Johnny Frenchman*, a wartime comedy drama about the rivalry between Breton and Cornish fishermen, which was to go into production in Cornwall, Patricia Roc came to mind. He approached Maurice Ostrer to see if he would release her. Ostrer was only too happy to loan her out to Ealing Studios for a one-picture deal, charging Ealing Studios £350 [£12,600] a week for a minimum of twelve weeks filming. But Ostrer would have none of it when Balcon expressed an interest in buying out her contract. She had sex appeal and sufficient acting ability that interested Balcon, but poaching her from Gainsborough wasn't to be, which is a pity – she would have slotted in well at Ealing and probably gone on to do bigger and better films.

Pat's co-stars in *Johnny Frenchman* were Tom Walls, who she had enjoyed working with in *Love Story*, French actress Françoise Rosay, and French Canadian newcomer Paul Dupuis. There was also another well know Ealing actor in the cast. His name was Ralph Michael. Cozied up in the secluded Trevalsa Court Hotel on the outskirts of Mevagissey, where the cast and main crew stayed during filming, presented the perfect setting for Pat and Ralph Michael to fall in love. Confessed Pat in later life; "I have only loved, really loved a few men in my life, and Ralph was one of them." The affair they embarked on whilst filming *Johnny Frenchman* was far more than 'a romp in the hay'. It lasted some considerable time, and was to lead to divorce from their respective spouses for both of them.

With fine aristocratic features and a cultured voice, Ralph Michael, whose real name was Ralph Champion Shutter, was a natural for the stiff-upper-lip roles calling for British reserve, something he wasn't too happy about because he found it restricting. Born in London in 1907, he had ten years stage experience before branching out into films, making his debut in *False Evidence* in 1937. According to Charles Barr in his book *Ealing Studios*, his persona was 'modest and unpassionate', which, for a screen hero, was somewhat limiting – as it was in *Johnny Frenchman*. His character is Bob Tremayne, a fisherman in Cornwall, whose boat 'Girl Sue' seems to interest him more than his fiancée, the local beauty Sue, played by Pat.

Yet again, Pat, described by P.L. Mannock of the *Daily Herald* as being 'self-consciously attractive', plays a young ingénue, 'sweet and sincere'. She is slightly worried that Bob hasn't shown any passion in wooing her, preferring instead a jokey relationship, like putting pilchards down her back. Little wonder then, that he loses her to Breton fisherman Yan Kervarec, played by the handsome Paul Dupuis.

It was a film which Pat particularly enjoyed making. She loved Cornwall and the Cornish people but was a tad disappointed by the finished film. For whatever reason, as an Ealing Picture production, *Johnny Frenchman* failed to reflect that studio's usually excellent standards. Some of the blame was the poor screenplay by T.E.B. Clarke, who would later find acclaim for writing some of Ealing's best comedies; *Passport to Pimlico, The Lavender Hill Mob, The Titfield Thunderbolt,* as well as one of Britain's best police films of the 1950's *The Blue Lamp*. Richard Winnington, writing in the *Evening Standard*, commented; "A film with an idea like *Johnny Frenchman* deserves to be as good and true as Carol Reed's *The Way Ahead*. It's a matter of script, script, script." *The Observer's* Caroline Lejeune thought that the film was a sketch for a good picture rather than a finished work. "The effects are lightly pencilled in; the execution is rough; the story, a romance between a Cornishman's daughter and a dashing Breton poacher, is of the slenderest; and the elegant attempts at some sort of rustic dialect are often painful," she wrote.

Charles Frend, who directed the film and later added *The Cruel Sea* and *Scott of the Antarctic* to his credits, must shoulder some of the blame for failing to please the critics. He failed to get the best out of the actors with perhaps one exception, that of Françoise Rosay, the grande dame of the French cinema, who was runner-up in the 1946 New York Film Critics' Awards for her portrayal of Lanec Florrie, the leader of the Breton fishing fraternity in the film.

As for the 'Cornish dialect', the only person to flavour his speech with something that is certainly not Cornish was Tom Walls, who incompletely disguises himself with a jersey and sea boots. He plays the harbour master Nat Pomeroy, the father of Pat's character who, according to Richard Winnington writing in the *News Chronicle*, 'wore a Kensington accent and idiom to match her Jacqmar scarf throughout much of the film.' Nevertheless, Pat did score with several critics. One of them, Patrick Kirwan, wrote: "Pat Roc does not merely rely on her undoubted good looks to carry her through the film. She acts with charm and sincerity."

Much of *Johnny Frenchman* was made at Mevagissey, a small Cornish fishing village which, with suitable scene changes, doubled as a fishing town in Brittany, France. Shooting began on 17 August 1944. "A few days later," recalled Pat, "news came through that the allied forces had liberated Paris and we gathered around the harbour and spontaneously sang *La Marseillaise*. It was lovely; there was so much camaraderie in those days," she added. By the time the film was premiered at the Odeon, Leicester Square in August 1945, world events had moved startlingly forward. Not only had the war in Europe been concluded, but a few days before the London opening, the atomic bomb had terminated the war in Japan. There was just time to update the ending of the film to refer to the victory.

In spite of the cool reception by the critics, the film did well at the box office and made the ten best films list in the fan magazine *Picture Show's* selection for 1945. Also in that list was *The Seventh Veil*, which starred James Mason. Mason thought highly of Patricia Roc, both as a friend and as an actress and, remembering her unsuccessful try out for *Hatter's Castle* three years earlier, suggested her for the role of Francesca, the young pianist who gets her knuckles wrapped by him in *The Seventh Veil*. The Academy Award winning original screenplay was written by Pat's friends Sydney and Muriel Box and she hoped for their support in her bid for the part. But Sydney Box, who personally financed and produced the film, was more inclined to the vague persona of Ann Todd. The film made Ann Todd an overnight success and brought her a lucrative Rank contract worth a quarter of a million pounds. It also led to an on and off screen affair of considerable passion between her and Mason. What might have happened, one wonders, had Patricia Roc been successful in landing the part, and would she have had the skill and ability to negotiate the difficult task of transforming a gauche, shy schoolgirl into an accomplished, sophisticated woman as Todd's charismatic performance did? Perhaps!

It wasn't the only time Mason attempted, unsuccessfully as it turned out, to get the name Patricia Roc alongside his in a film. A few months later he tried hard to persuade Carol Reed, the producer and director of *Odd Man Out*, that his lover, Ann Todd, would be very good as Kathleen, the girl who shelters Mason's character and finally gives her life to die with him during the gunfight in the snow. When Reed rejected her, Mason then put forward Patricia Roc, but she was, in the eyes of Carol Reed, not suitable either. In the end Kathleen Ryan, the Irish stage actress making her film debut, got the nod from Reed. Regarded as one of the great British films of all time, *Odd Man Out*, which won the British Film Academy's award for best British picture in 1946, was another important acting opportunity that Pat lost.

Back home from Cornwall, Ralph Michael moved into Pat's Hallam Street flat with her, which didn't go down well with his devastated wife, the distinguished actress Fay Compton, sister of the novelist and playwright Sir Compton Mackenzie, whom he had married two years earlier. Hurt and humiliated, she conveniently 'leaked' the story of her husband's infidelity to the press as an act of revenge.

***

Writing in 2000, Dame Thora Hird recalled an evening when her husband, through a coded message, told her over the telephone that he was being posted abroad. She was appearing at the time in the play *No Medals* in London's West End with Fay Compton. "I went to the side of the stage", wrote Dame Thora, "ready to go on feeling a bit sad. George, the doorkeeper, must have told Miss Compton about my telephone conversation, and just as I was about to go on, she said to me, quite kindly, 'I believe your husband has gone abroad and left you on your own.' Unfortunately I said, 'Oh yes. But I'm not the only one am I Miss Compton?' I didn't know that the *Evening News* had just come out with a big picture of Fay's husband, with the headline that he had run off with Pat Roc. I was meaning that many women's husbands were being sent overseas. She said, 'No – you're not the only one. And he hasn't left you for a chorus girl, has he?'"

The *chorus girl's* bosses were not at all happy with the cozy arrangement of Ralph Michael cohabiting with Pat, and it is no coincidence that she was hastily packed off on a nation-wide tour to promote her latest Gainsborough films, *Love Story* and *Madonna of the Seven Moons*.

Not wanting to jeopardise her career, she eagerly embarked on the tour accompanied with a dresser and hairdresser as well as publicity aides. Endless travelling between towns and cities may have been demanding, but it was certainly gratifying because it was then that she realised just how popular she really was. "I was amazed at the crowds of autograph hunters and people who just came to get a glimpse of me. It gave me a very warm feeling," she said.

Michael Thornton remembers, as a schoolboy, seeing her when the tour took her to Brighton. "She was mobbed by a crowd of several thousand people," he recalled, adding, "One would have had to have seen this to realise what a gigantic idol she was."

"They said I always held Pat as if she were a time bomb." Gordon Jackson and Patricia Roc in a scene from 'Millions Like Us' (ITV Studios Global Entertainment)

Pat getting direction from Frank Launder and two unidentified technicians during filming 'Millions Like Us' (Courtesy of Brian Twist)

Pat with Moore Marriot who plays her father in 'Millions Like Us'
(ITV Studios Global Entertainment)

Pat in her Hallam Street flat in late 1946
(Courtesy of Michael Thomas)

Margaret Lockwood, Stewart Granger and Patricia Roc in headscarf and dungarees, clutching a cigarette, but still managing to look appealing in a scene from 'Love Story' (ITV Studios Global Entertainment)

Confrontation time! Pat and Margaret Lockwood in a scene from 'Love Story' (ITV Studios Global Entertainment)

Wherever Pat went, there was always an adoring crowd to greet and meet her. Here she is in 1946, signing autograph books whilst celebrating her third place in the 'Daily Mail's National Film Awards (Author's Private Collection)

The main cast in 'Johnny Frenchman' from left: Tom Walls, Francoise Rosary, Paul Dupuis, Pat and Ralph Michael (Author's Private Collection)

CHAPTER SEVEN

The Wicked Lady and Hollywood

'WHAT does the future hold for this talented actress?" agonised fan magazine *Picturegoer* about Patricia Roc. "A succession of 'other women' parts or soppy heroines? Or is she really going to be treated seriously as she deserves and given a starring role with the other characters subordinate to her?" it went on. Alas, the bosses at Gainsborough weren't listening, casting Pat yet again in a supporting role to Margaret Lockwood. The film was the infamous *The Wicked Lady*, another of Ostrer's period costume extravaganzas. He instinctively knew that the story - that of sex, romance and violence - was exactly the sort of fare that the cinema going public wanted at that time – and he was right. Produced by R.J. Minney, and directed and adapted from Magdalen King-Hall's novel *Life and Death of the Wicked Lady Skelton* by Leslie Arliss, *The Wicked Lady* became one of Britain's most all time popular films.

Without doubt, this was yet another Margaret Lockwood film. She got the plum part, that of the villainous Lady Barbara Skelton. In total contrast, Patricia Roc was cast as Caroline the 'good' girl, who is humiliated and manipulated by her so called best friend Lady Barbara. On the eve of Caroline's wedding, Barbara steals her fiancé, the hapless Sir Ralph Skelton (Griffith Jones). The broken-hearted Caroline, who has been trying on her wedding dress, wants to leave at once, but Barbara humiliates her still further by telling her she must stay and act as the chief bridesmaid to save her lover's face. Caroline agrees and tearfully offers Barbara her wedding dress. "Wear that, I wouldn't even be buried in it!" Lockwood tells the audience in a contemptuous aside.   As the story develops, the *wicked* Lady Barbara plots her new husband's murder, seduces Caroline's new fiancé and commits highway robbery with notorious highwayman Jackson, played by James Mason. Stewart Granger was first offered the part of Jackson, but turned it down, something he later regretted, because there wasn't sufficient dialogue.

The way Caroline allowed herself to be manipulated by Barbara prompted film historian Robert Murphy to describe Patricia Roc's character as 'insipid, spineless and rather silly.' This was not however, what director Leslie Arliss had in mind. "Far from being just another spineless kind of role, Caroline is a strong character in spite of her apparent weakness in giving in to her rival. Her will power is strong and once roused, she puts up a good fight against the powerful Lady Skelton," he explained. Inevitably overshadowed by Margaret Lockwood, Patricia Roc still manages to transform what might have been an unpromising role into a portrayal of a woman who matures through experience, and who has learned to turn the system, which constrains her, to some advantage. The problem was, it took most of the film's 103 minute running time before Caroline became 'roused', when faces, yet again, were slapped between Pat and Lockwood. In Pat's own words: "The character infuriated me. She was a saccharine-sweet little ninny who stood back and allowed another woman to snatch her lover. The only time I had any respect for her was when she lost her temper and walloped Margaret Lockwood."

Predictably, the critics subjected *The Wicked Lady* to critical scorn. Take for instance *The Manchester Guardian*'s verdict that it was 'an odd mixture of hot passion and cold suet pudding'. But despite the barrage of disapproval, *The Wicked Lady* was a great hit with the public and was the highest grossing film in Britain in 1946. 'Three years after its release the film had been seen by 30 million people and had grossed more than £1 million [£29,000,000], a record no other film, British or American, could match', wrote Hilton Tims in his book *Once a Wicked Lady*. And its popularity continued. When, in 2004, the British Film Institute looked at cinema ticket sales since the dawn of the talkie, to create the all-time list for the most popular films in the country, *The Wicked Lady* came in ninth place, beating heavily hyped films such as *Harry Potter and the Philosopher's Stone, Grease,* and *Jaws.*

"I loved making *The Wicked Lady*, we had such fun, it was just gorgeous," said Pat. "We did the exteriors at that wonderful house in Norfolk, Blickling Hall, such a beautiful house. I thoroughly enjoyed working on that film. And it was a joy working with Maggie. I adored her. I remember we used to try and out-do one another with our antique jewellery. We both collected it, and would spend hours around the junk shops hunting for a bargain, and try and wear any new 'finds' in the film if we could."

The premiere of *The Wicked Lady* at the Gaumont, Haymarket on 19 November 1945 was somewhat controversial. It was to be held in the presence of 87 year-old Queen Mary, the proceeds going to charity. The critics, who had already seen the film at a press preview, had pronounced it too 'bawdy' and 'immoral' for the royal eyes and ears. A special viewing for one of the Queen's equerries was hurriedly arranged in the afternoon, just hours before the performance, for his opinion. Thankfully, for J. Arthur Rank, Maurice Ostrer and some of the most powerful men in the film industry, the equerry gave the film his approval. The gatherings of journalists present at the premiere were hoping that the Queen would show signs of disapproval and would walk out in a huff. Instead, she congratulated Margaret Lockwood telling her "That was a very good film – I enjoyed it very much."

Most of the cast connected with the film were present at the premiere, with two notable exceptions. James Mason was touring Germany, entertaining the troops, with his wife Pamela Kellino. As for Pat, she was 6000 miles away making a film in Hollywood, where she planned to celebrate the occasion by throwing a party for her new friends out there, 'in honour of the gallant people of the British studios who braved the blitz to keep the industry going during the war'.

A very solemn looking Patricia Roc in 'The Wicked Lady' when she thinks that she has lost the man she loves for good. In the film she is supposed to sings 'Love Steals Your Heart' but it was Millicent Phillips who provided the voice. (Courtesy of Michael Thomas)

Leslie Arliss started planning a sequel to *The Wicked Lady* but J. Arthur Rank vetoed it. He was quite happy with the first film in which the 'wicked lady' got her comeuppance and conventional morality was satisfied, but he wasn't prepared to exploit it with a further outrageously immoral film.

At the beginning of 1982, it was reported that film director Michael Winner planned a remake of *The Wicked Lady* based on Leslie Arliss's original script, with Faye Dunaway in the lead part and Glynis Barber, better known for playing Det. Sgt. 'Harry' Makepeace in the hit TV series *Dempsey and Makepeace*, taking on the role of Caroline. It was hinted that both Pat and Margaret Lockwood were to be offered cameo roles in this remake, but nothing came of it. They were, however, invited to the film's premiere in 1983, but both wisely declined. Neither wanted to be associated with what turned out to be an even more camp version than the original, updated with bare bosoms and humping couples. Pat wasn't very complementary about the remake and said that at the time people were saying that Faye Dunaway had 'Dunaway' with her career; it was that bad!

Amid much publicity, it was announced that Patricia Roc would be the first British star to go to Hollywood under J Arthur Rank's ill-fated lease-lend scheme with Universal Studios. It was a part of Rank's ambitious plan to expand his cinema interests worldwide, and in particular the United States, where he considered he could best reap the profits from his home produced films for future investment and production. Pat's role in this ambitious plan was as an ambassadress, the hope being that her performance as a British star would help to increase the appeal for British pictures by American audiences.

She seemed the obvious choice, especially as Margaret Lockwood refused to set foot on American soil after her dismal pre-war experiences, when she played second fiddle to nine-year old Shirley Temple in *Susannah of the Mounties*. As for Phyllis Calvert and Deborah Kerr, they were reluctant to go at all, resisting all offers until late 1946, when the war could no longer be offered as a valid excuse for declining.

But in any case, J Arthur Rank thought highly of Pat. When, for instance, in 1946 he celebrated the re-opening of Pinewood studios with a number of his contract players, he insisted on Pat being next to him. To Rank, she represented everything that was good about the British film industry. She had beauty, intelligence and elegance - class without the airs, which showed in the many characters she played on screen. Apart from that, Hollywood film producer Walter Wanger, who, in 1951, notoriously served a two year prison sentence for shooting his wife Joan Bennett's lover in *the balls* when he caught her cheating on him, was so impressed by Pat's tender performance in *Millions Like*

Us that it was he who suggested to Rank that she would be ideal to play the part of Caroline in *Canyon Passage*, a film he was producing for Universal about the 1850s pioneering days in Oregon.

It all seemed a cosy and plausible arrangement, but there was of course another reason why Rank was anxious for his favourite contract star to be out of the country at that time. He was anxious to protect both her and his movie empire from the impending publicity of her divorce from Murray. The divorce laws in the 1940s dictated that the easiest way to gain a divorce was to establish that one of the partnership had committed adultery. Pat's husband had plenty of evidence that Pat had been unfaithful and decided to divorce her on the grounds of adultery. In his petition he cited Ralph Michael as co-respondent, although any number of others could have been included, Michael Wilding for one. Even more damaging for Pat's career, naming her as co-respondent, Fay Compton served divorce papers on her toy-boy husband Ralph Michael, thirteen years her junior. Both petitions were scheduled to be heard at the High Court in December.

In a period when the British film industry was on a 'high', any sniff of a scandal would have threatened to end the career of one of Rank's most popular and lucrative actresses, as well as cast a dark shadow over his film empire. It was felt all-round that it would be best if Pat were kept well away, out of the public eye. Yorkshire man, J. Arthur Rank, who made a considerable amount of *brass* from his Rank Hovis McDougall flour business, was a devout member of the Methodist Church and had distinctly narrow-minded views about contemporary issues - views shared by his chief executive and henchman John Davis, a dauntingly cold and authoritarian man of whom Patricia Roc vehemently commented, "I haven't a good word for him." Both Rank and Davis expected their contract stars to toe the moral line and avoid any scandal that might jeopardise the puritanical image they were trying to establish within the Rank Organisation, of which Gainsborough was a part. This was rich, given Davis's five marriages and unsavoury divorce cases including a somewhat messy divorce from actress Dinah Sheridan, whose son Jeremy Handley - for a short time Chairman of the Conservative Party during the Premiership of John Major - sang *'Oh What a Beautiful Morning'* on the day in 1993, when it was announced that Sir John Davis, as he was then, had died.

With Pat out of the country, both Rank and Davis were hoping for damage limitation and they weren't too disappointed. The divorce hearing on 21 December 1945 at the High Court was straightforward and passed relatively unnoticed, the press attaching little significance to the petition Laing *versus* Laing. And besides, in the 1940s, the press boys, with whom Pat had a very good working relationship, were far less intrusive into the lives of stars and celebrities than they are by today's standards.

However, the divorce hearing between Virginia Lilian Emmeline Shotter and Ralph Champion Shotter, to give Fay Compton and Ralph Michael their married names, wasn't heard until Monday, February 11. Pat had intended returning from Hollywood after filming *Canyon Passage* was complete on the Queen Elizabeth on 5 February which meant that she would have arrived back home just as the hearing was about to be heard. Instead, she wisely decided to stay put to give the divorce scandal time to quieten down, on the pretext of having her teeth recapped in America at a cost of $2000, about the equivalent of £16,500 in 2013, something she said British dentists were incapable of doing satisfactorily!

The Rank Organisation had tried hard to dissuade Compton from citing Pat in her petition, but she was out for revenge, no doubt hoping that both Pat's and her husband's careers would be damaged. To her delight, the day after the hearing, most of the British newspapers reported the divorce, as did those as far away as Australia. In Britain for instance, *The Daily Mirror* story read:

> Two well know actresses figured in an undefended action in the London Divorce Courts yesterday (11 February). Patricia Roc was cited by Fay Compton who was granted a decree nisi.
>
> Miss Compton's case was that her husband Ralph Champion Shotter (Ralph Michael) met Miss Roc while making a film in Cornwall. On returning to London he told Fay Compton he had fallen in love with Miss Roc, and admitted misconduct. Miss Compton later discovered that her husband and Miss Roc had stayed together in her flat in Hallam Street, London. Miss Compton who is 51 has been married four times.

Career-wise, Pat's did suffer in the short term. Whilst she was filming *Canyon Passage* she was interviewed by W. H. Mooring, the Hollywood correspondent for *Picturegoer*, and told him that she would have to return to London soon after Christmas to start a new film for Gainsborough. That picture was *Diggers Republic*, a story about a Salvation Army girl and a mine prospector. Preparations for the film, which was to have been made on location in South Africa by Leslie Arliss, with Stewart Granger as Pat's co-star, were well in hand. However, as a direct result of the divorce, Pat was dropped from the cast, and the project eventually mothballed until 1949, when Sydney Box resurrected it, giving the film the new title *Diamond City*, with Honor Blackman and David Farrar replacing Pat and Granger.

Ralph Michael's career suffered even more. He was under contract to Ealing Studios, but following the two divorce hearings, his and Pat's, he was dropped by the studio and never made another film for Ealing after completing *The Captive Heart* in 1945. In December he followed Pat out to America hoping to pick up some work there and rekindle his affair with her, but after 12 months and failing on both counts, he returned to Britain, married actress Joyce Heron and made a successful career on television, making his last appearance on the small screen in a episode of the P.G. Woodhouse series *Jeeves and Wooster* in 1993, the year before he died.

'Good Luck Bunny' – the photograph Ralph Michael gave to
Pat during their passionate love affair. (Courtesy of Michael Thomas)

As for Murray Laing, he remained in the Mayfair flat and married Dr. Antonia (Toni) Charlotte Izod in 1949. He moved, with Toni, to Henley on Thames in 1984, where he spent the last four years of his life, dying in November 1988. Pat never said whether she kept in touch with Murray after the divorce but it seems unlikely. They had their marital rows like most couples, but they became more frequent after Pat had met, and had fallen in love with Michael Wilding. Murray hated Pat's flirtatious behaviour and was constantly suspicious of her goings-on, and with good cause. It seems that he never forgave her and even returned the photograph she had given him in 1941.

The photograph Murray Laing returned to Pat when they divorced.
(Courtesy of Michael Thomas)

Pat went to America on 17 August 1945, two days after completing her work on *The Wicked Lady*. Flying across the Atlantic in a seaplane and taking the best part of a day to get there, she spent her first night in Baltimore, where she was given Maryland chicken for dinner. "It was the size of a house," said Pat, who couldn't get over the waste of food. "Unbelievable! I thought it was terrible after the rationing we had back home", she told Henry Jaremko.

From Baltimore she went to New York by train, and was met by the American showbiz hacks who loved to' bait British actresses for their hoity-toity naiveties. One photographer hollered: "How about some cheesecake?" Pat instinctively thought he meant the rich cheese pastry tart. "I'd love some" she replied and sat back to wait for it to arrive. Then she was conscious that he was staring at her in an odd sort of way. "Well!" he said. "Well!" she countered. She then discovered that "cheesecake" in film parlance was anything but the edible type. He was waiting for her to raise her skirt for a leg picture!

She made other faux pas whilst she was in America, calling the carpenters 'chippies' which, until she explained, they were not too pleased about. She also had a lot of explaining to do when she decided to take a nap and asked one of the studio managers to come to her dressing room at four in the afternoon to 'knock her up'. "In Hollywood they couldn't wait for you to have a scandal", she recalled, "and if they couldn't find one they made it up and printed it in the *Hollywood Reporter* anyway".

"What," asked *Picturegoer*, "will Hollywood do to Pat Roc?" when the magazine learned of her proposed trip to the USA. Her many fans feared that she might not even return to Britain at all if she proved a success out there. But they need not have worried. To her relief, she found that instead of wanting to change her personality, Hollywood insisted that she should remain '100 per cent English Pat Roc'. Her *very* English demure persona was exactly what Hollywood wanted. And as for staying out there, Pat only made the one film in America.

Canyon Passage cost $2.3 million to make, and turned out to be Wanger's most successful post-war film both financially and aesthetically. But it wasn't so for Pat, even though she was paid £7000 [£238,000] plus an additional $200 a week living expenses whilst she was in Hollywood. She was fourth billed behind Dana Andrews, Brian Donlevy and free-lancing Susan Hayward, the actress who went to Hollywood in 1937 and unsuccessfully tested for the much coveted role of Scarlett O'Hara in *Gone With the Wind*. Pat plays the part of Caroline, the fiancée of Dana Andrews' character, Logan, but loses him to

Lucy, played by the feisty Hayward.

Susan Hayward, who took her husband, actor Jess Barker, and their six-month old twins Timothy and Gregory on location with her, completely dominates the picture as far as the female roles were concerned. If that worried Pat it didn't show. She really liked Susan Hayward and got on well with her. "Susan was a down to earth, no nonsense girl, qualities I admire in a person," said Pat. 'No nonsense' was right. At one stage during filming Hayward's temperament caused her to aggressively protest to Walter Wanger that the director, Jacques Tourneur, wasn't shooting enough close-ups of her. In a cable to Wanger, telling him that she was 'the star vehicle', she complained:

THOUGHT MOUNTAINS AND CLOUD STUFF BEAUTIFUL. DEEPLY DISAPPOINTED AUDIENCE DID NOT SEE THIS EMPLOYEE'S FACE. AS LONG AS WE'RE TO BE HIRED TEN MORE DAYS WOULD APPRECIATE IF YOU WOULD ORDER RETAKE OR CLOSE-UP. WANT TO DO BEST POSSIBLE JOB BUT WANT IT TO BE SHOT SO AUDIENCE GETS WHAT YOU PAY ME FOR.

Canyon Passage was based on a *Saturday Evening Post* story by Ernest Haycox, who had earlier written the classic Western *Stagecoach*, filmed in 1939 by John Ford. The main character, Logan, transports cargo by packhorse between the 'booming' trade town of Portland and unsettled Jacksonville. During one of these trips his close friend Camrose (Brian Donlevy) asks him to take his fiancée, Lucy, from Portland to Jacksonville to join him there. It is patently obvious that Logan is in love with Lucy but avoids her out of loyalty to his friend and courts instead Caroline.

Pat's character is an English girl whose father was killed by the Indians. She lives with nearby settlers, Ben Dance and his wife (Andy Devine and Dorothy Peterson). It is when Camrose is killed during an Indian attack, that Logan and Lucy are free to love each other. Poor Caroline, like her character in *The Wicked Lady*, is dumped before she reaches the alter. But she is not too unhappy about it. She realises that she would never have been truly happy with the restless Logan and settles for Ben Dance's eldest son Bushrod (Denny Devine, the son of Andy Devine) who has quietly been in love with her from the first day she arrived in Jacksonville.

With singer Hoagy Carmichael providing comic and musical relief with his song 'Ole Buttermilk Sky', receiving an Academy Award nomination (losing out to the catchy song 'On the Atchison, Topeka and the Santa Fe', featured in *The Harvey Girls*), the film was generally well received by the critics. "A brilliantly engineered movie," wrote the *Time* critic. But it didn't come alive for Pat. In November 1946 when the film went on release in Britain, *Picturegoer* said; "Patricia Roc in her first American picture is nicely served with the role of Caroline, although it is only a secondary part. But she makes a definite impression, and a good one." But six months later the magazine revised its opinion, saying; "Patricia Roc's debut was not too successful. The picture was dominated by Susan Hayward and Patricia Roc has little chance to show her real acting ability." Given the chance, perhaps Pat could have offered a better performance, but her role was undemanding; the material just wasn't there for her, even though Wanger build up her part as the picture progressed. A slightly condescending Susan Hayward, who actually liked Pat and spent a lot of time with her, reportedly told the American press, "That limey is one hell of a dame. She sure can act".

Regardless of performance, Patricia Roc was the darling of the studio whilst she was in Hollywood. Rose Hobart who played Martha Lestrode, a gambling woman in love with Donlevy's character in the film, said of her, "Patricia was so lovely to look at and so genuinely endearing to the whole crew from director to the last prop man," a sentiment that was endorsed by David Niven. "The whole studio fell in love with Patricia Roc when she was making *Canyon Passage* at Universal Studios," he recalled whilst reminiscing with author Sheridan Morley.

There was somebody else who fell in love with Patricia Roc, and that was America's future president, Ronald Wilson Reagan. He had just completed a four-year stint working for the Army Air Corp's Motion Picture Unit, when Pat arrived in the States. At the time, he was married to actress Jane Wyman, but she now had little time for him. She was busy building a career that was to gain her an Academy Award for Best Actress in 1948 for her role in *Johnny Belinda*. In contrast, his film career was heading nowhere. After his discharge from the forces he wrote in his autobiography *Where's The Rest Of Me*? "All I wanted to do was to rest up a while, make love to my wife and come up refreshed to do a better job in an ideal world. As it came out, I was disappointed in all these post-war ambitions." It didn't help Reagan when Warner Brothers, who had him under contract, offered him $3500 weekly to sit around doing nothing. That wasn't Reagan's style; he was an active man with an active brain. Jack Warner told him, "Just relax until we find a good property for you." It took the best part of seven months for that to happen. After just a few weeks without working, and his wife almost totally ignoring him, Reagan became deeply depressed, began drinking heavily and was on the verge of a nervous breakdown. He began to think of, and talk about suicide.

The photograph of Pat with Ronald Reagan which was
always on display in her drawing-room
(Courtesy of Michael Thomas)

Fortunately for Reagan, and as it transpired for America too, he got to know Pat. Always a very buoyant lady, with a distinct sunny disposition, she unquestionably boosted his self-esteem with her presence, and generally talked some valuable sense into him, sense which he valued for the rest of his life. Reagan's biographer Bob Colacello wanted to include this episode of Reagan's life in his book *Ronnie and Nancy: The Long Climb, 1911- 1980,* but decided to drop it when Reagan's widow, Nancy, complained that it made her husband look weak and unfaithful in marriage, and did not accord with her views of him. That is not surprising; no self-respecting American would want to think of their President in such a way.

Pat first met Reagan at one of Hollywood's show biz restaurants The Brown Derby, where Walter Wanger had taken her for lunch on her second day in Hollywood. He wanted to discuss the film she was about to make, and to get to know her a little better. Sitting at the next table was Ronald Reagan and fellow actor Adolphe Menjou, talking endlessly about Communism and 'Reds under the beds'. Wanger advised Pat to steer well clear of him. "He's the biggest bore in Hollywood," he told her.

Eventually, even Menjou had had enough. He made his excuses, got up and left Reagan sitting at the table alone. Wanger too, had to leave the lunch early to attend a studio conference. Pat insisted on staying and joined Reagan at his table. His affable smile and warmth won her over immediately. But as she got to know him better she realized that he was as heartbroken and devastated as a man could be. "He was just wretched and miserable," she said. "He adored his wife and family, and just couldn't understand why or how she had completely lost interest in him. Had I been older I suppose I would have realised that he was suffering a sort of breakdown as he was quite often in tears, and dangerously depressed. He several times told me: 'Life just isn't worth living any more. I just don't see the point of going on'. I became deeply fond of him," Pat went on, "but rather as one becomes fond of a lost child. We became lovers because quite frankly, I was scared and lonely on my arrival in Hollywood, and sex seemed the only thing to alleviate his utter misery. I was seriously concerned that he might do something to himself if I didn't make him feel that somebody wanted him, because his wife sure as hell didn't. Of course we had to be extremely careful how and where we met, especially as he was still locked into one of the highest profile marriages in Hollywood. We could both have lost our contracts had we been caught out," she said.

Regardless of Nancy Reagan's views on this episode in her husband's life, there is little doubt that Ronald Reagan fell in love with Pat. He followed her everywhere, even on location. "I couldn't turn round without falling over him" she said. "If I went out to dinner with another man, he would tip the waiters to get him a table next to mine where he would sit alone and stare at me. He was very sweet but when he was in love, he did tend to look like a sick parrot". It is doubtful that Pat was truly in love with him, nevertheless, throughout her life she prominently displayed in her drawing-room a photograph of the two of them together in a loving pose. "The past is not something I want to hide", she said. But neither was it something she wanted to dwell upon. She was always a very private person and extraordinarily discreet and reticent about sexual matters. Only after she died did her relationship with Ronald Reagan surface.

Reagan wasn't the only man to take a fancy to Pat. There were several who were only too eager to be seen out with her during her time in Hollywood. She was regularly on the arm of Cary Grant, Errol Flynn, Brian Donlevy, Lloyd Bridges, and many others, including Ward Bond who had a gargantuan crush on her. Within days of Pat arriving back in England he sent her a cable:

THE MORE I SEE AMERICAN WOMEN THE BETTER I LIKE LIMEYS. EITHER YOU GET ME IN YOUR NEXT PICTURE OR I'LL GET YOU IN MINE OR MUST I COME THERE TO SEE YOU. UNCLE WARD

`Uncle Ward` was how Pat always referred to recently divorced Ward Bond. Born in 1903, he regarded John Ford, one of Hollywood's best known, best loved, and most sort-after directors, as his closest friend. When Bond died in 1960, aged fifty-seven after a massive heart attack, Ford went up to Andy Devine during the funeral service telling him, "Now YOU'RE the biggest asshole I know."

Also a regular on Pat's dinner date list was the Academy Award winning sixty-eight-year-old actor Charles Coburn, who certainly had an eye for pretty young girls. In his autobiography *My Word Is My Bond*, Roger Moore recalls the time when Petula Clark, still in her teens, sat on Coburn's knee as he sang 'It's a long long while from May to December', as his hand, much to her disapproval, slowly moved from her knee up her leg to the hem of her skirt. Pat never disclosed whether Coburn 'sang' to her!

But there was one person in particular who was seen out with Pat more than anybody else and that was Charlie Prince. Prince was an artists' agent and was assigned to Pat during her stay in Hollywood to look after all her contractual publicity events and personal appearances. He had started his career in the film industry as an uncredited film extra in 1937 playing in *Blossoms on Broadway, Thanks for Listening, Sea Devils*, and *The Devil Diamond*. Not making much headway as an actor, he decided to go into star management, and joined the E.T. Somlyo agency in South Canon Drive, Beverly Hills, where Cary Grant also had an office. Prince was an eight-handicap golfer and spent a lot of his time at the Lakeside Golf Club, a club for the rich and famous whose membership included Bob Hope and Bing Crosby. He also rented an apartment there. His name could always be found on the playing list with most of Hollywood's stars at charity golf tournaments, which even if he didn't win, was invariably high up the leader board.

Pat's first date with Prince was on 13 November, when she returned from the Oregon location, dining at the fashionable Beachcomber in Beverly Hills. From then on she seemed to be rarely out of his company and was frequently seen with him at the Lakeside, where she accompanied him when he played in various Motion Picture Golf tournaments. When it was time for her to return home, she was reluctant to leave him but her immediate work was in England – or so she thought - and she was still under contract to Gainsborough. Together they flew from California to New York where they spent two final days, and nights, together before saying their last goodbyes, determined that the 'goodbyes' weren't going to be forever.

CHAPTER EIGHT

Back to England and a Frosty Reception

FILMING for *Canyon Passage* came to an end on January 15. For the next seven weeks before she returned home Pat was the British movie star living the glamorous life in America, attending star-studded parties, wearing gorgeous designer clothes and making love passionately and often. She so loved being treated like the *goddess of the Odeons,* cosseted and pampered like royalty and so ardently pursued. It certainly helped take her mind off the sticky situation she would face back in England. But all good things inevitably come to an end, and on 3 March 1946 Pat set sail for Southampton, travelling first class on the *Queen Mary.* Even though the ship was still under military command and used to carry GI brides from Europe to America, it was still lavishly decorated in the VIP quarters.

During the six-day voyage, flowers would be delivered daily to Pat's private cabin from Charlie Prince with notes telling how much he missed and loved her. There is no doubt that she was sad that she had to leave America, yet happy that she had fallen in love with `a wonderful man` whom she was not likely to forget in a hurry. She told W. H. Mooring whilst she was still in Hollywood, that she had planned big changes in her private life. Could this have been anything to do with her relationship with Prince?

When the *Queen Mary* docked on Saturday 9 March, there was no 'welcome home 'party as there had been when Margaret Lockwood returned from Hollywood. Instead, Betty Box, the sister of Sydney Box who was soon to replace Maurice Ostrer at Gainsborough, travelled to Southampton to meet Pat off the boat, and broke the news that J.D. (John Davis) wanted to see her in his South Street office in Mayfair on Monday morning. Pat didn't think much of Davis at the best of times, and instinctively knew that she was in for a rough time. The meeting was 'frosty' to say the least as Davis laboured on about Pat's affair with Ralph Michael, and how she had damaged the studio's strict family-values policy. He then informed her that whilst she was not being placed on suspension, it would be best all-round if she didn't make any films or go on any promotional tours, until the scandal of the Compton divorce had had time to die down.

In the meantime, Gainsbourough exercised its option for Pat's services for a third year, starting on 1 March 1946. Normally she would have signed the agreement without too much delay but on this occasion she weighed up her options, and kept her bosses waiting until the following August before she put pen to paper to confirm that she would continue with her seven-year contract. Pat felt let down, especially as she had been flying the Rankery (Sir Donald Sinden's pet name for the Rank Organisation) flag in America for the past six months.

There was also another consideration. J. Arthur Rank, who had been content to pursue a hands-off policy since acquiring Gainsborough Pictures in 1941, was dissatisfied with Maurice Ostrer's output of less than three films a year from that studio. Consequently, three weeks after Pat arrived back in England, having been increasingly and systematically isolated by the flour magnate, Ostrer resigned from Gainsborough, the company he had helped to create eighteen years earlier.

Pat was a little wary of the change and how it would affect her. She had always liked Ostrer, she knew where she stood with him and had a certain empathy for the man who frequently took her into his confidence. While she was in Hollywood for instance, he rather indiscreetly wrote to her, voicing his displeasure that Rank had sided with Margaret Lockwood when she refused to appear in his production, *The Magic Bow*. Hinting that from now on Pat would be his number one star, Ostrer said that he didn't intend to use Margaret Lockwood ever again and that after her next film he guaranteed she would start to go on the downgrade quickly. Lockwood didn't go *downgrade* of course, and Pat never got to reap the benefits of Ostrer's plans for her. When he left Gainsborough, he took R.J. Minney with him. Together they formed an independent production company, Premier Productions, and engaged Leslie Arliss to direct their one and only film, *Idol of Paris*, to the Gainsborough formula of bodice-ripping flamboyance. Ostrer failed in his attempt to recruit the services of Pat for the film, which is just as well because it failed miserably at the box-office, prompting Ostrer to quit the film business for good.

Having been away so long, Pat had a lot of catching up to do with her friends. There was no particular man in her life, apart from Charlie Prince, but he was thousands of miles away. Her parents now lived in Bray, by the river Thames where Pat spent a lot of time on her return from America. She mulled over with her father the possibility of returning to the stage. It was, after all, what she had wanted to be - a stage actress rather than a `film star'. It was an idea she also discussed with Cary Grant when she had dinner with him one evening. He had just finished filming Hitchcock's *Notorious* and was in England visiting his mother who still lived in Bristol. He came up with a better idea. Acting as 'go between' for Charlie Prince and Pat, he persuaded her to follow her heart and return to America to see Charlie again to try and sort out her future. It had now been several weeks since they said their goodbyes at the New York dockside, and Pat was not taking the separation well.

Whether Pat had already thought of going back to America so soon after leaving, who can say. But now that the seeds had been sown in her mind, she wasted little time arranging her flight, having had J. Arthur Rank's blessing to take a few days off. If the truth be known, Pat would have gone anyway, with or without Rank's permission. Having been side-lined by Davis, she was not scheduled to make any films for them in the foreseeable future, and she still hadn't committed herself to a further year at Rank.

On 14 May 1946, flying with American Overseas Airlines, Pat boarded a Douglas C-54 Skymaster at Hurn Airport (now known as Bournemouth Airport) bound for New York where Charlie Prince was eagerly awaiting her arrival. After unlocking themselves from one another's arms, they took a cab to the Savoy Plaza Hotel, one of the priciest hotels in the city, where they shared an apartment. Pat's brief but poignant diary entries for these few days of her life make interesting reading:

Friday May 17 `Happier than ever`.
Sunday May 19 `At hotel, so happy`.
Monday May 20 `Danced at Waldorf Starlight Roof. Will marry my love`.
Tuesday May 21 `Born yesterday, adore my Charlie`.
Thursday May 23 `Return to London. Made up my mind to marry CP`.
Saturday May 25 `Phoned Lakeside Golf Club, "Charlie I love you"` `.
Sunday May 26 `Wrote Charlie - lonely for him`.
Sunday June 16 `Wrote 2 letters to Charlie. Love him so much`.
Sunday 30 June `Phoned Charlie, "love you so much my darling"'`.

Pat had done it again – she had fallen hopelessly in love!

When she returned home from her week of sheer delight in New York, she was undecided about her future. If she married Prince it would mean her leaving England to live in America, as her sister had done ten years earlier. On the other hand, she enjoyed the aura of star celebrity in Britain and all that it offered. A further consideration was the fact that she was not working. She didn't know if she still had, or even wanted a career at Rank. Determined to sort out her dilemma once and for all, a meeting was arranged between Pat, her agent Eric Goodhead, and J. Arthur himself. She gave him it to him straight. "Put me to work in films or *the goddess* will leave for America." It was a dangerous game she was playing but one which she won. The outcome was that Rank offered to give her a present of £2,000 [£68,000] to compensate her for the idle time enforced on her by John Davis. He also promised that she would not be without work for very much longer. As it turned out, 1946 was one of Pat's busiest years, and one of her most lucrative. During the last six months of 1946 she made no fewer than three feature films, often working simultaneously on all three, travelling between studios to complete scenes in each.

The decree nisi granted to Murray Laing against Pat was made absolute on 1 July 1946, which meant that she was now free to marry Charlie Prince if she chose. She eventually chose not to. The relationship between the two hadn't lasted the summer out. The huge distance separating them didn`t help, but that wasn't the only reason. For the time being Pat had sorted out her career to her satisfaction, and more significantly, she had met a new man in her life. His name was David Macdonald.

In the meantime, there was the equivalent of the American Oscars to attend in London. Whilst Pat was in America making *Canyon Passage*, the *Daily Mail* launched its annual National Film Award to mark the golden jubilee of the cinema in Britain, and to give the millions of people who attended the cinema every week the opportunity of choosing their favourite British film and stars. It was decided for the first year that voting would be for the entire film output of six years of the war. For three weeks the cinemagoers voted for their favourites. When the results were announced on April 25, Pat was delighted to learn that she was voted third most popular actress behind Margaret Lockwood and Phyllis Calvert. James Mason won the actor's award and *The Way to the Stars,* which starred Michael Redgrave and John Mills, was the most popular film.

On a warm summer evening in June the crowds literally packed Park Lane to welcome the stars as they arrived at the Dorchester Hotel for the presentations. Judging by the rapturous welcome the crowd gave Pat as she stepped out of the limousine and waved to them, you would have thought that she was the out and out winner. But this enthusiastic welcome was not unusual for the star who had endeared herself to the British people the way that Pat had done. And it certainly dispelled any notions John Davis had, that the cinema going public would turn its back on her because of the Compton divorce case.

She was now receiving more than five thousand fan letters weekly, mostly wanting autographs and photographs, but there were some fans with different requests. She was once sent an Indian Ghurkha-knife by a former Chindit major, asking her if she would autograph it by carving her name on the handle. Then there was one letter from a teenager who invited Pat down to Devon for the weekend. "If it is fine", he wrote, "We could cycle to Exeter, it's only fifteen miles".

"I would trade your memory only for that of the loveliest English rose," wrote another of her fans. Such popularity, hitherto reserved for the biggest Hollywood stars, was undoubtedly down to her star persona. In the early days as a Gainsborough contract player, she had always gone out of her way not to appear too glamorous or aloof, prompting Noël Coward to say of her: "She is a phenomenon, an unspoilt movie star who can act". Coward was a good friend to Pat. He gave her a lot of valuable advice and once told her, as he did to many of his friends in the business, "Never turn a job down, no matter how small it is, because if you are not working, you are not acting."

Not everyone shared Coward's opinion about Pat's acting ability. "Pat couldn't act for toffee apples," Dulcie Gray told Matthew Sweet in 2005, adding, "But she was beautiful. She was a very clever girl who knew her limitations exactly, and didn't give a damn about them. She was no fool." Dulcie Gray, who was married to Michael Denison for fifty-nine years before his death in 1998, was more associated with the theatre than with films and her remarks were typical of a stage actress. Nevertheless, they were not shared by Jean Kent, one of Pat's contemporaries at Gainsborough and who, during her career, appeared in four films with her. She thought Gray's assessment of Pat's acting ability to be ` a load of rubbish`. "Pat was a lovely actress and had great natural charm. She always kept everything simple and didn't overplay any scene", she said.

Asked how she approached acting, Pat said: "It seems to me that if acting is meant to portray life, it is a good idea to live normally. So often a good part is ruined by the technical perfection of the acting, and the complete absence of real emotion."

Maurice Ostrer's successor at Gainsborough was Sydney Box. He was appointed managing director by Rank on the understanding that he would increase the studio's production to twelve pictures a year. The appointment was made largely on the strength of *The Seventh Veil*, the film Box made as an independent for less than £100,000 [£34,000,000]. Not only was it a phenomenal success, breaking box-office records in both London and New York, but it also won him and his then wife Muriel Box, (who after their divorce in 1969 married Lord Gardiner, Lord Chancellor in the Labour administration in the 1960s) an Academy Award for Best Original Screenplay.

Before Box took up his new appointment on 1 August, his independent production company Triton was busy finalising arrangements for *The Brothers*, a story of clan rivalry and sexual jealousy set in a remote Scottish community in the early 1900s. The film was to be directed by David MacDonald. Born in Scotland in 1904, and trained in Hollywood under the watchful eye of Cecil B de Mille, MacDonald graduated to film director when he returned to England in the 1930s, where he came into contact with the novelist L. A. G. Strong. In 1936 the two of them made an agreement that they would make a film of Strong's 1932 novel *The Brothers* whenever the conditions were right. Following demobilization, after a distinguished wartime career as head of the Army Kinematograph Unit and director of some notable documentaries, MacDonald approached Sydney Box as the most likely person to take on *The Brothers*. Box enthusiastically agreed to produce the innovative historical drama and cast Ann Todd to play the central character of Mary Lawson, the young Scots orphan, sent to be a servant-girl in the croft of Hector Macrae and his two sons, Fergus and John. It was only after Ann Todd threw a dramatic tantrum and refused to be in the film that Sydney Box, turned his attentions towards Pat. He knew her current dilemma, and not having any film commitments thought she would jump at the chance to replace Todd.

Pat was now a far more confident person - some would argue, rebellious - following her American trip. Seeing how things got done over there and no doubt heeding the advice her American counterparts had given her, Ronald Reagan and Ward Bond in particular, she was now determined not to get `pushed around` and to make some important decisions of her own. The studios were seeing a different side to a much tougher Pat, one that alienated some of the top producers high up in the Rank group. They decided that she was getting temperamental following her trip to Hollywood. Show-biz writer Eric Braun, and at one time, publicist for Peter Sellers, Beryl Reid, Michael Dennison and Dulcie Gray, used to say that the two most difficult stars of the late 1940s era were Valerie Hobson and Patricia Roc.

The meeting she had with J. Arthur Rank must have given Pat, or so she felt, certain bargaining powers, powers she wouldn't have dreamt of exercising in the past. No longer was she prepared to accept the namby-pamby roles as she had done in the past. She felt that she was now ready to play `real women`. However, after being overlooked by Box for the part in *The Seventh Veil* in favour of Ann Todd, she must have had the feeling that she was being offered leftovers - films Todd didn't want to do. Instead of jumping at the chance Box offered her, even though she realised that it was without question the best dramatic opportunity she had been offered in her entire career so far, Pat told Box that she would discuss it with her agent before coming to a decision.

"Sparks have flown in all directions...Sidney has suspended Ann Todd's contract because at the last minute she backed out of her part and Pat Roc had to be <u>persuaded</u> into taking her place", wrote Muriel Box in her diary for 2 July. Just how Sydney Box persuaded Pat is not known; maybe he offered her top billing with her name above the title, which is how the film was presented when it was released. Or, more likely it was the £5000 [£170,000] fee he promised her if she would do the film, which was far more than she would have received under the terms of her contract. Whatever it was, Pat in her wisdom realised that there was a good chance that *The Brothers* would be a big hit at the box-office, and that would inevitably consolidate her star status once and for all.

Having finally accepted the part of Mary Lawson, Pat left London in mid-July for The Isle of Skye where most of *The Brothers* was filmed. When she and the rest of the company disembarked from the short ferry ride from Kyle of Lochalsh to Kyleakin, they were met by a large gathering of inquisitive islanders, many of whom were later hired as extras. They were also greeted by the bearded, larger-than-life locations manager, none other than James Robertson Justice, who was yet to make his name playing Sir Lancelot in *The Doctor* series of comedy films. Robertson Justice. Standing there, suitably dressed for the occasion in full Highland regalia and looking for the entire world like the local laird, Pat and the rest of the crew instinctively knew they were in for a good time, and that's just what she had. Whenever asked which film role she enjoyed most, Pat always, and without hesitation, chose *The Brothers*. "I choose it without question because there is nothing I should like more than to relive those glorious eight weeks we spent on location in Skye," explained Pat. "It was truly wonderful, and before we left Skye the islanders organised a dance for us in the village hall and piled us with gifts, ranging from deliciously cured kippers to Shetland shawls made by the local women. It was magical,"

In the film, Mary Lawson is a pretty orphan brought up in Glasgow, who, in 1900, is sent to live with the Macraes on the Isle of Skye. Her unfamiliar charms soon ensnare the sons of two feuding families, Willy McFarish, played by newcomer Andrew Crawford, and Fergus and John Macrae, the brothers. As the feuding intensifies, the film ends in a number of deaths including that of Mary herself, which was contrary to the happy ending Strong had written in his original story. Typical of Sydney Box, he believed that cruelty paid good commercial dividends, and was heavily criticised by the critics for it.

For Pat, it was a role not unlike the one she had played in *Johnny Frenchman* where she engendered rivalry between a Breton and a Cornish fisherman. But whereas her appeal in that film was as a modern, town-bred girl, in *The Brothers* she lacked the emotional range of Mary Lawson, in which she needed to be both femme fatale - something she always maintained she could never be because of the shape of her face - and victim. In fact, there are times when she appears artificial and out of place in the primitive world of Skye. Ann Todd and her fragile, witch-like beauty would have made a much better Mary.

The casting for the film turned out to be a case of musical chairs. Originally, Sydney Box wanted Emlyn Williams to play `John` and Michael Redgrave for `Fergus`. First Williams dropped out. He was replaced by Eric Portman. Then Redgrave decided that he would prefer to appear in *Fame is the Spur* for the Boulting Brothers, and was hastily replaced by Maxwell Reed. In the meantime, the notoriously difficult Eric Portman refused to do the film with Box's original choice, Ann Todd, and was replaced by the splendidly malevolent Duncan Macrae. When Ann Todd learnt that Maxwell Reed had been cast to play Fergus, she refused point blank to appear with him again. Having been knocked about by Reed in the controversial film *Daybreak*, which had its release delayed by two years because of censorship problems, Todd had no intention of allowing herself to be again, whipped, wooed and finally murdered by the big clumsy Irishman, whose acting, according to Patricia Roc, was somewhat limited. "He was not a great person to work with quite frankly", said Pat. "He was never really in the part. He just stood there and sort of, well he didn't show any emotion at all." Muriel Box was in agreement. "It was a mistake casting Maxwell Reed. He was still very inexperienced and lacked the emotional expressiveness needed for the role," she said.

Maxwell Reed died in 1974 when he was 55. Modelling himself on Stewart Granger, he appeared in a number of films, and became a bit of a matinee idol because of his good looks - the Rank publicity department called him 'The Beautiful Beast'. In 1952 he married eighteen-year-old Joan Collins The marriage was a fiasco from the start and much to Joan Collins' relief, they divorced four years later when, claimed Collins in her autobiography *Past Imperfect,* he allegedly tried to sell her to an Arab sheik.

It is doubtful if Pat and Reed had any sort of sexual relationship during the making of *The Brothers*, but it is difficult to believe that Reed, a practised womaniser, who was four years younger than Pat, never tried to lay a finger on her. If he did indeed make advances she would almost certainly have rejected them. She was now being ardently courted by David MacDonald, something which didn't go unnoticed by the rest of the crew. 'Go to bed alone,' was the knowing comment Duncan Macrae wrote in Pat's autograph book.

By now Pat was used to the innocuous publicity duties that followed the films she had just made. On this occasion the *Scottish Daily Mail* had organised a series of concerts for 1947 which aimed to provide a radio link for Scots living abroad. The first of these concerts was broadcast in January from Glasgow's Odeon Cinema. Pat joined the programme that also featured Will Fyffe, Duncan Macrae, Gordon Jackson, Robert Wilson, the pipe and drums of the Highland Infantry Training Corps from Edinburgh and Joe Loss and his orchestra, though it is difficult to imagine what his claim to Scottish nostalgia might have been. Whetting the appetite, Pat, Fyffe and Macrae performed excerpts from *The Brothers* which was not yet on general release.

It was the last time Pat saw Will Fyffe. A few months later he died, aged 62, after falling out of a second storey window at his own hotel, The Rusacks, which overlooks the 18th green at the St. Andrew's golf course. He had been working on the film *Bonnie Prince Charles* with David Niven when he became ill after contracting an ear infection. Following a small operation he went to St Andrews to recuperate. "He was a character," mused Pat when recalling her Gainsborough days. "Committed suicide, didn't he? Threw himself out of a window, or so I heard," she said. The coroner recorded a verdict of `accidental death`.

*Patricia Roc on her arrival at
Grand Central Station, New York
on her way to Hollywood.
"How about some cheesecake?"
the photographers asked – but
Pat was having none of it and
confidently stood her ground!
(Author's Private Collection)*

*'Introducing Patricia Roc', the
movie poster outside the
Marquee in Times Square, New York
(Courtesy of Michael Thomas)*

*Relaxing at Diamond Lake, Oregon, the location site for 'Canyon Passage'.
Left; Lloyd Bridges, Dana Andrews. Ernest Haycox, Pat and Andy Devine.
(Author's Private Collection)*

*Make –up director Jack P. Pierce give some last minute adjustments
to Pat's locket during the filming of 'Canyon Passage'.
(Authors Private Collection)*

109

Patricia Roc on board the Queen Mary homeward bound from Hollywood.
(Courtesy of Michael Thomas)

CHAPTER NINE

1946 – A very busy year

STILL finishing off interior scenes for *The Brothers*, Pat reported to Denham Film Studios to start work on the adaptation of James Hilton's novel, *So Well Remembered*, the first of a proposed series of Anglo-American co-productions between Hollywood's RKO Radio Pictures and the Rank Organisation. The film, narrated by Hilton, is about an idealistic newspaper editor trying to improve conditions in his factory town between the two World Wars. It is a good hour before Pat's contribution as a nurse during the Second World War emerges. But whilst she attempts to make the most of the smaller part she has been given, *So Well Remembered*, which starred John Mills, Trevor Howard, and Americans, Martha Scott and John Carson, did little to further her career, even though it was in the top ten highest grossing British pictures in 1947. It did however enhance her bank balance by £3000 [£100,000].

Because the director Edward Dymtryk and producer Adrian Scott, whose earlier collaborations included the 'film noir' classic *Farewell My Lovely*, were being scrutinised by Hollywood Red-baiters at the time, the film suffered unfair accusations that its attitudes were Communist-inspired. The year of the film's release, Dymtryk and Scott became members of the infamous 'Hollywood Ten' and were sentenced to one-year jail terms for refusing to testify before the House Un-American Activities Committee. With the ironic title of *So Well Remembered*, the film was buried by the Americans and for many years vanished without trace. But in 2004, one lone copy was found in the States, and was digitally enhanced and issued on video and DVD. It was one of the few films that Pat never got to see in its entirety.

One of her films that she did see, and enjoyed, was the adaptation of Norah Loft's novel *Jassy*. It was produced by Sydney Box, who gave Pat a much better chance to shine in what was to be the last `official` Gainsborough costume drama. As head of the studio, he wanted to leave the overworked costume melodramas of Maurice Ostrer behind, and open up a wider variety of material. But faced with having to make 10 to 12 films a year, his first priority was to put the studio space to work. He had inherited from Ostrer just one script, that of *Jassy*, in any state of readiness for filming, so Box reluctantly decided to press ahead with it, in order to buy time before new scripts became available. However, if he were to make it, then it would be, he decided, the finest of its genre - an elaborate last flourish for the cycle, with lavishly designed sets by the four times Oscar nominated Maurice Carter. "I was given the biggest budget I'd ever had for sets. It was the first Gainsbough film ever to be photographed in colour too, which made it more challenging for me, but I enjoyed working on that film," said Carter. Box also needed a strong cast and the obvious choice was to reunite Patricia Roc and Margaret Lockwood in the leading roles.

Neither showed any enthusiasm to return to the tired old formula, and besides, Pat was busy finishing off interior scenes at Shepherds Bush for *The Brothers*, still shooting scenes at Denham for *So Well Remembered*, as well as embarking on a publicity tour. But when Box explained his problem, they both agreed to do it. Pat, who was usually associated with sexual restraint (at least in her films) stipulated that she didn`t want to be the `good girl` again. She wanted to be the villain of the piece, even though she knew that that would mean playing second fiddle to Margaret Lockwood for a third time. Box hoped that James Mason would play the part of the sadistic gambler, but that was a bit of wishful thinking. Mason had moved on, already having vowed after *The Wicked Lady* never to get caught up in any of Gainsborough`s costume bodice-rippers again. Instead, the affable Basil Sydney was cast in that part, and was refreshingly unsympathetic, even though, recalled Margaret Lockwood, he was a bit of a giggler. "It was like being back at school. In some of our most dramatic scenes, we'd crease up laughing and couldn't carry on," she told Hilton Tims in his book, *Once a Wicked Lady.*

Before production of *Jassy* got underway in September, Pat had been called back to Islington to re-shoot certain scenes of *The Wicked Lady* for its American release because the straight laced Hays Code, which protected the morality of cinemagoers in America, irrationally objected to the over exposure of cleavage shown by Pat and Margaret Lockwood. The Breen Office, which was responsible for Code enforcement, was ever vigilant, but inconsistent if you consider the scantily dressed Betty Grable and June Haver in the American film *The Dolly Sisters*, which slipped through their own censorship organisation's net the same year.

"Americans do not want half naked women like Patricia Roc in this movie" screamed the headlines of the American Press. The fact that the dresses, designed by double Oscar winner Elizabeth Haffenden, were historically correct for the period, seemed of little importance to the Americans. They regarded them far too exciting for their cinema audiences, especially when the two stars' bosoms bounced around almost uncontrollably when they were riding in the coach over cobble stone streets, to see James Mason hang at Tyburn. Rank, and most of the people in the British film industry, knew only too well of course that it was part of a campaign to keep popular British films out of American cinemas. But Rank, gleefully exploiting the publicity, out-witted them by re-shooting all the daring parts again. "It wasn't easy," recalled Pat. "Apart from covering up, we had to duplicate gestures and expressions exactly as we had done twelve months earlier, but I think the boss was pleased. Hardly a day went by", she said, "without receiving a bouquet of wonderful flowers from an appreciative Sydney Box."

On 16 October Pat reported to the Gainsborough Studios to start work on *Jassy*, a gypsy-to-gentry uninhibited melodrama set in the 1830s fictional Mummerset. It gave Margaret Lockwood plenty of scope to be strong willed, but little to behave badly. That role fell to Patricia Roc who was at her most bitchy, and whilst on the one hand is kind and sweet, on the other, behaves appallingly towards both Margaret Lockwood and newcomer Dermot Walsh. He plays Barney, Pat's love interest, who, with a touch of déjà vu, finishes up in the arms of Lockwood. The critics were slightly snooty about the clichés, the mixture-as-before aspect, the rambling plot and the lack of conviction, but the cinema going public loved it. It was a run-away success at the cinemas throughout Britain and one of the highest grossing pictures in 1947.

In November, the annual Royal Command Film Performance was inaugurated, with Michael Powell and Emeric Pressburger's *A Matter of Life and Death* being the chosen film. It was certainly a night to remember, with more than five thousand fans gathered outside the Odeon Empire cinema in Leicester Square to see King George V, Queen Elizabeth, the two Princesses and the stars arrive. Patricia Roc, her hair still in long ringlets from the day's filming on *Jassy*, looked stunning in a mink bolero over her evening dress. She received a tremendous welcome from the waiting crowd and proved equal to any of the Hollywood stars who had flown in specially for the occasion. They included Walter Wanger with his wife Joan Bennett, in London for the British

113

premiere later that month of *Canyon Passage*.

As the year came to a close, Pat had one last film assignment to fulfil, playing herself in Gainsborough`s *Holiday Camp*. In the film she was cast as "Patricia Roc - film star", one of the judges of a beauty competition at a Yorkshire holiday camp, where most of the picture was filmed. Pat devoted half a day playing the part, and was rewarded with a fur coat for her efforts by Sydney Box.

When Pat returned home from her stint in Hollywood she not only had to face the fallout from the Compton divorce case, but the tirade from John Davis too. Her immediate future looked bleak to say the least. But as it happened, 1946 turned out to be the most successful in Pat's entire career; certainly as far as financial rewards were concerned. By today's monetary standards she earned in excess of half a million pounds, rivalling the top Rank stars of the day, Stewart Granger and James Mason. Not only that, her bosses realising that *the goddess* was still very popular with the cinema goers – in other words, she put bums on seats – they launched the Patricia Roc International Fan Club magazine in December. Membership cost four shillings, which entitled the fans to an autographed photo of Pat and twelve issues of the monthly magazine (this was reduced to six issues when the magazine went bi-monthly in 1948).

Pat was on a high – everything seemed to be going her way. There was only one downside as far as she was concerned; her *fella* David Macdonald had to fly to Italy on 15 December to shoot location scenes for *Snowbound*, the film he was making for Gainsborough, which meant that they missed spending their first Christmas together. Charlie Prince, it would seem, was but a distant dream.

In love yet again, on 3 November Pat wrote in her diary, 'Say `yes` to Davie' which almost certainly was a response to a marriage proposal even though Macdonald was already married to a lady he had met in Hollywood some years earlier.

"Davie home today I hope" Pat wrote in her diary for 29 December. And he did return on the twenty-ninth to a warm, a very warm reception from Pat, but a bitterly cold London.

CHAPTER TEN

1947 – A Very Strange year

THE first icy blast of winter came on the 23 January 1947, when snow fell heavily over the south and southwest of England. The blizzard in southwest England was the worst since 1891; many villages in Devon were cut-off and even the Scilly Isles were blanketed with snow. Temperatures started to plummet throughout the country. On the night of the 28th, -20.6 °C was recorded in Essex and the following night, -21.3 °C in Kent. It was so cold that Big Ben started missing beats.

It was in this miserable cold weather that Pat started shooting her next picture, *When the Bough Breaks*, a social realism film in which she plays a hapless single parent. The film was made at the old Gainsborough Studios in Islington, known by the film technicians as 'the warren'. The producer, Betty Box recalled, "We had not only the coldest winter I think we had ever had, but there was also a fuel shortage and power cuts the whole time. I had to hire a generator from a fairground, which we parked in the road outside the studio, to provide electricity for studio lighting so that we could go on shooting, else we would have had to stop and that would have cost us £1000 [£30,000] a day. We all froze, but we carried on. I remember working with poor Patricia Roc who had to wear little cotton summer dresses. But she didn`t grumble and we finished the film on schedule".

Pat`s co-star and love interest was Bill Owen, now remembered for his role as the loveable rascal Compo in the long running television comedy series *Last of the Summer Wine*. Recalling those bleak conditions he said, "There was only a one bar electric fire in the studio which artists were supposed to share, but only if they could squeeze past Pat and me."

Owen, who was an inch or two shorter than Pat, and had to wear lifts in his shoes, admitted that playing opposite Pat wasn't really his scene, as the critics confirmed. "Bill Owen must have been as surprised as we are to find himself playing a romantic lead" wrote one, with the *Monthly Film Bulletin* adding, "It is strange that so unromantic a person as Bill Owen was chosen for Pat Roc's male lead. He makes the shopkeeper a nice little fellow, but Patricia Roc's fans will feel cheated of their ration of a heartthrob".

The story is about a young woman, Lily Bates, played by Pat, who finds, after giving birth to her son, that the father, to whom she thought she was married, has been arrested for bigamy. Finding that she is now a single mother, (quite scandalous at the time when the film was made) Lily puts her baby into a nursery so that she can go job hunting. Frances Norman, a nursery helper played by Rosamund John, develops a strong bond with the child, who is called Jimmy, and offers to look after him when Lily gets the flu. When she recovers she goes to collect young Jimmy but, realising that he would be much better off living with Frances and her husband Robert, (Patrick Holt) she suggests that they adopt him. They eagerly agree having just lost their own baby.

Some years later, Lily meets and marries a respectable suburban shopkeeper called Bill Collins, (Bill Owen), and now wants her child back. Because no formal adoption papers were ever drawn up at the time, Lily is granted custody of Jimmy. After a short time with his real mother, Jimmy, now a ten-year-old, cannot settle and runs away to be with his adoptive parents. Lily capitulates and agrees that the boy must return to the Normans. The film ends with Lily finding out that she is pregnant. "I always did say so", said Bill. "Say what?" said Lily. "I always did say it would be easier to have one of our own."

The British Board of Censors was reasonably tolerant, but frowned on the very mention of 'bigamy' in the film and gave it an "A" certificate instead of the "U" certificate which producer Betty Box was anticipating and hoping for.

Writing forty years later, film historian Robert Murphy in his book, *Realism and Tinsel,* thought that `Pat Roc is at her best as the insecure working-class mum who can't relate to her child`. But at the time, most of the critics slated the film and even worse, panned Pat's performance. *The Observer's* critic Caroline Lejeune thought that the film was; "a supreme example of imbecility, acted for all its worth by Misses P. Roc and R. John, and for rather more than it is worth by a young man called Bill Owen." *Kinematograph Weekly* was even more damning, claiming, "Patricia Roc fails to put much evident feeling into the role of Lily Bates. Her acting range is very limited." Leonard Moseley in the Daily Express was no kinder; "If you go and see *When the Bough Breaks*, you will do well to leave your adult brains in the cloakroom for it is obviously made for filmgoers with the mental age of nine. Or perhaps I'm flattering it. Patricia Roc and Rosamund John, neither of whom could claim to be the most demonstrative actresses in British films, play the thwarted mothers with rather a hunted air, as if they suspected that something was wrong but weren't sure what."

Muriel Box, who co-wrote the screen script with her then husband, Sydney Box, wrote in her diary:

"*When the Bough Breaks* came in for an appalling bad press. Described as the worst film of 1947. It will be interesting to see how far bad (press) stories can effect a film when it goes on general release".

The *Daily Worker* critic was one of the few who gave the film a good review, saying; "A woman producer is responsible for the British film surprise packet of the year...If it were French it would probably be hailed as a masterpiece. Pat Roc, shedding her usual mantle of glamour, is surprisingly good as a working girl...It is the way Miss Box (the producer) and director Lawrence Huntington have handled this tricky moral problem which lifts the film right out of the common rut, and should reap big dividends at the box office." It did do quite well at the box office, making a reasonable profit for Rank, which isn't too surprising seeing that the film was made for less than £125,000 [£4,000,000]. Even Pat's entire wardrobe was bought `off-the-peg` from an Oxford Street store and cost less than £25 [£800].

The role of young Jimmy was played by eight-year-old Cavan Malone, the son of 1930s popular Irish singer, Danny Malone. "He was such a nice little boy," said Pat. "Always willing to listen and learn, and very polite. I was very sad when I heard that he had died when he was quite young." Cavan died from heart failure in 1982 when he was forty-two. Working with Pat was his first acting job, and he did well for a newcomer. But stardom never beckoned, abandoning his acting career in the early 1960s when he stood trial for murder. He was eventually acquitted, pleading that the man he killed was attacking his mother, Hazel Malone, one of the co-founders of the Corona Stage Academy. From acting, Cavan turned his attention to the drums and became one of Britain's top drummers, playing at one stage with the Geraldo Orchestra.

When visiting show business journalist Robert Stannage interviewed Pat whilst she was making *When the Bough Breaks,* she told him that that she would

117

have little opportunity for a rest because she had two pictures lined up for 1947 – *The Reluctant Widow*, and *The Killer and the Slain*. As it happened she made neither. *The Reluctant Widow* was delayed for two years, and by that time Pat had moved on and was living in Paris and no longer under contract to the Rank Organisation. Jean Kent gratefully accepted the role Pat was to have played in Georgette Heyer's Victorian mystery story about a French governess who marries an English Lord.

By 1947 Pat had become a household name. Here, Giles the 'Daily Express' cartoonist cashes in on her and Margaret Lockwood's popularity to promote the paper's Annual Film Ball at the Royal Albert Hall. (Daily Express, 28 September 1947)

The Killer and the Slain, an adaptation of Hugh Walpole's controversial psychological thriller about a murderer who gradually turns into the man he has killed, was to have starred Eric Portman, with Pat playing his wife, Eve, but the film never got made. After spending £15,000 [£465,000] preparing the production, including commissioning a screen play by Bridget Boland and hiring Henry French to direct the film, the Rank board cancelled it, depriving Pat of a marvellous acting opportunity. They claimed that it was too sadistic and gloomy for present day audiences.

The Killer and the Slain having been axed, Sydney Box thought that Pat would jump at the chance to appear in his film *Broken Journey*, a story about a plane that crashes in the Alps. He thought wrong! When she learnt that she would yet again be subordinate to Phyllis Calvert, the star in the film, she was furious. She contacted Eric Goodhead and told him that she would not do the film at any cost. She felt that she deserved better and was no longer going to be cajoled into accepting secondary roles just for the sake of pleasing her bosses. In her mind she had been far too docile, far too even-tempered, far too agreeable for most of her film career. It was time to unveil the new Patricia Roc; an actress commanding top billing, and not some foil for the likes of Lockwood and Calvert.

Box was not pleased with Pat's refusal, but he let it pass which is more than he did a few months later, when he placed Margaret Lockwood on six months suspension. She refused to appear in his film, *Roses for her Pillow*, retiled *Once Upon a Dream* when it was released in 1948 with Googie Withers as her replacement.

With no immediate film commitments, Rank could not afford to leave Pat idle for long. They sent her off on yet another personal appearance tour around the proveniences where the fans seldom got the chance to see stars in the flesh. It was a routine chore, one of the basic duties of being a film star, but Pat was as enthusiastic as ever. Travelling like Royalty, she set off with an entourage of dresser, hairdresser, publicity aides and of course, Theo Cowan, Rank's head of publicity, 'the life and sole of the party'. A typical itinerary when she visited the Potteries for instance, included signing the visitors book for the then Lord Mayor Harry Beresford; personal appearances at two cinemas, 'The Regent' at Hanley and 'The Coliseum' at Burslem; meeting the workers at the Paragon China works in Longton and to cap it all off, attending the famous Cinema Ball organised by the North Staffordshire Branch of the Cinematic Exhibitor's Association, the most glamorous fixture in the city's social calendar during the 1940s

"It was very tiring doing the rounds, but Theo was marvellous company and kept us amused the whole time we were away", said Pat. Cowan, tall and good looking was well known in the industry for his sense of humour. He first became a publicist in 1936 for Gaumont-British Pictures and after war service joined Rank. His job there was to look after the public image of Rank's stars when they were away from the studios. 'Generally looking after them' was his own job description...organising the logistics of personal appearances, attendances at premières, charity events, garden parties and promotional tours like Pat's.

Pat always enjoyed Cowan's company and assured Margaret Lockwood when she was sent by Rank on a promotional tour with Cowan a few months later, that there wouldn't be a dull moment. And there wasn't, far from it. During that tour, Lockwood and Cowan became romantically involved, which developed into a full-blown affair lasting several months.

Back home after the tour, Pat was still on publicity duty. In June, she judged a beauty competition with Trevor Howard and her lover at that time, David MacDonald, as her fellow judges. Over 30,000 Joe Lyons' employees saw Pat select Lily Layton `Miss Lyons 1947` and present her with the 'Patricia Roc Trophy'. The whole purpose of these outings was to promote the stars' latest films and besides *The Brothers*, Pat and Howard were no doubt promoting the film they did together, *So Well Remembered*. Like Pat, Howard considered such jaunts important and always took the time to publicise his films. He said:

"It's all part of the job. You always find some actors who say 'I got paid only for making the film, so let the studio publicise it.' But I've always thought that actors are the best resource a film company has to publicise a film. Besides, if you want the public to come and see you as often as they'll tolerate you, you must make the effort to do more than just make films you'll hope the public will like. You must promote them."

Howard's thoughts sum up Pat's philosophy too. "I loved to go up and down the country meeting the fans and telling them about my latest picture" she said. And no matter where she went, she always received a rapturous welcome, being one of few stars at the time who could relate to the general public in a way that they could warm to. Her secret, if it was a secret, was to blend in with her fans as much as possible. She went out of her way not to appear too glamorous or aloof and whilst she was attractive to men, she was also unthreatening to women. Even in her fan magazine she adopts a confidential tone in her 'personal letter' as though she is writing to a pen pal. In the December 1946 issue for instance she wrote:

'I suppose you are wondering how I am going to spend Christmas? Well I'll let you into a secret. I shall be spending it in a lovely house in Bray with my father, my sister Marie-Louise and her husband and their one-year-old son, Brian

Anthony. Unfortunately, Mummy and my eldest sister `Bobby` are in Hollywood, but I am arranging to make a transatlantic `phone call to wish them a Happy Christmas. Having let you into one secret, I'm going to disclose another. For many years I have kept an autograph book in which most of the famous people I have met have written a message. Next month I hope to print some of these messages so that you too can share my autograph book. It is one of my most prized possessions and I always keep it in my dressing room at the studio so that I can 'hook' any distinguished visitors.'

Having whiled away most of the early summer travelling up and down the country making personal appearances and judging beauty competitions, Pat was at last cast in her next picture. It follows the misadventures of a young English woman Mary Santel, Pat's character, and her dog called 'Floppy', and an Italian singer Giulio Moris, played by the Italian operatic tenor, Nino Martini. Both have become stranded overnight, without money or luggage, on an Italian railway station. Inevitably, romance blossoms. Called *One Night with You,* an adaptation of Carlo Ludovico Bragaglia's Italian musical comedy *Fuga a due Voci,* many considered it to be an English version of Frank Capra`s highly successful 1934 film, *It Happened One Night,* which starred Claudette Colbert and Clark Gable. However, before Pat reported to Denham studios to start work on the film there was one more publicity assignment she had to fulfil.

When she returned from Hollywood, she enthused so much about the 'publicity machines' of the studios out there, that the head of Gainsborough publicity, Tom Burdon, started to think on similar lines. The outcome was that she embarked on a special four-day photo shoot, resulting in 650 photographs of her, all in different poses, which found their way into publications of every type the world over. Even today, a lot of them are still being offered, and eagerly sought after, on the Internet auction sites.

At the time, it was an ambitious programme. It was the first of its type ever carried out in Britain, and took the ten-man self-contained unit and Pat through Oxfordshire and Buckinghamshire. "I remember it well," said Pat. "I was photographed against fourteenth century cottages, village greens, picturesque country gardens, fishing for trout, swimming, cycling, with dogs, meeting village children – you name it, we did it. It was four days of tremendous fun and was a huge welcome change from the eternal studio backdrops and gilded carvings and white satin *chaise longue* normally used for our publicity photographs."

Billed as 'the first comedy with music to come from Two Cities Films to fill the need for lighter entertainment', *One Night with You* featured a number of excellent British character actors, including Bonar Colleano, Guy Middleton, Stanley Holloway, and Richard (Mr. Pastry) Hearne. Also in the cast, making his second film, was graduate from Rank's 'charm school', twenty-five-year-old Christopher Lee, who achieved stardom when he appeared as the monster in *The Curse of Frankenstein,* made by Hammer Films at Bray in 1957.

In September 1947, Pat, with the rest of the cast, went to Northern Italy for a month to begin filming. They were based at the holiday resort Stresa on Lake Maggiore. But one 'actor' who had to stay at home because of the quarantine laws was Floppy, Pat's champagne Pekingese, who has a most important role in the film. In fact, he is responsible for the whole story. He did his 'acting' at Denham, where, on the very last day of his contribution, he ran out into one of the busy studio roads and finished up with a broken leg.

The film was directed by Terence Young. His long career in British cinema encompassed a variety of genres and international co-productions, but he is probably now remembered as the director of the first two James Bond films, *Dr No,* and his own personal favourite, *From Russia With Love,* arguably the best in the entire series of *Bond* films. Young began his film career as a screenwriter in British films during the 1940s, before trying his hand at directing. During the war he was a tank commander, and was wounded in Arnhem during 'Operation Market Garden'. He was nursed back to health by a sixteen-year-old Belgium girl called Audrey Heenstra, who became better known as Audrey Hepburn.

Terence Young and Pat, both the same age, became good friends. He was intelligent and witty, and made Pat laugh. They got on well together which prompted the gossipmongers to put the word around that the two were having an affair. When Young's wife, the novelist Dorothea Bennett, got wind of the story, she stormed round to Pat's flat one evening and slapped her hard around the face, screaming at her as she did, "leave my husband alone".

Young assured his wife that the reports of an affair were untrue, telling her that whilst he enjoyed Pat's company enormously, they were not romantically involved, but she wasn't convinced. She was all too aware of 'the bedrock's' reputation. In an attempt to get Dorothea to back off, Young encouraged Pat to go out with his friend, André Thomas. She didn't know it at the time, but he would eventually become her second husband.

André Thomas, who was the director of lighting and photography on *One Night with You,* got on well with Young, having worked with him in France, when Young directed *Corridor of Mirror,* they became close friends. Born in Plouaret, France, in 1911 and educated in Paris, Thomas started his film career in 1931 and continued making films in Paris during the German occupation. When he became involved with Pat, little did she realise that he was a married man. In 1939 he had met and married a young English dancer from Newcastle called Lilian Padden, who bore him a daughter, Yannick Thomas, in 1942. After André had met, Pat, Lilian realised that she had lost her husband's affections, and that their marriage was over. She divorced Thomas in 1948, left France, and moved back to London and eventually settled in New York with her daughter.

Thomas spoke very little English, making his friendship with fluent-in-French Pat particularly pleasurable. Reading between the lines, it seems as though Pat found it 'particularly pleasurable' too. In her fan magazine, she wrote after the film had been completed:

'I hope you all enjoy *One Night With You* as much as I enjoyed making it. I think I enjoyed making it more than any other film. Perhaps because I was in such a happy frame of mind all the time, and perhaps because the film is a gay light-hearted one – the kind of picture we all want to see in these difficult times.'

Pat may have enjoyed making the film, which went on general release on 7 June 1948, but the critics were none too keen. "The comedy is stodgy and dismally slow. Patricia Roc as Mary, gives a disinterested, completely characterless performance, but André Thomas's photography is excellent", wrote the *Monthly Film Bulletin's* critic.

Within days of completing *One Night With You,* Pat was heading for Pinewood Studios to start work on her next picture, *London Belongs to Me.* Budgeted at £230,000 [almost £7 million], filming began on 6 November and was scheduled to take 14 weeks to complete. However, Pat caused several big wigs at Rank to bite through their big fat Havana cigars when, after two weeks of shooting scenes with her co-star Richard Attenborough, she walked out of her role in the film. "If I'd been consulted about the part in the first place, I certainly wouldn't have accepted it," said an angry Pat, adding that she wouldn't be 'caught' in such a spot again. The 'official reason' put out by the Rank Press Office quoted Pat saying, "I want to play a role in which I can be glamorous, wear lovely clothes and express a sense of humour. In *London Belongs to Me* I play a Cockney part, and I was tired of Cockney parts."

Is it really credible that Pat, an experienced actress, would have agreed to play the part of Doris Josser without knowing that she was being cast as a working-class girl, as she claimed? Hardly! It was when she learned that Fay Compton, the woman who called Pat a 'chorus girl', and now the ex-wife of Pat's one-time lover Ralph Michael, had been cast to play, of all people, her mother in the film, that Pat had serious misgivings about the outcome. Sidney Gilliat, the director and co-writer of the film script, assured Pat that everything would be fine and promised to keep a close eye on the delicate situation. But it wasn't, and he didn't. According to Thora Hird, Fay Compton could be a very mean and bitter woman and quite disruptive too, even getting thrown out of Denville Hall, the home for retired actors, when she went to live there because of her troublesome behaviour. She certainly wasn't in a magnanimous frame of mind when the two women had to act their first scenes together. Compton made Pat's life hell, complaining to the director about Pat's poor acting ability, her inaptness for the role, and generally humiliating her in front of the rest of the cast and crew. Pat was unable to fight back and after two weeks, having had enough, walked off the set, much to Compton's satisfaction.

According to Bobby, Pat's sister, the Attenboroughs really helped Pat through this difficult time and gave her a lot of moral support. But when asked to contribute his recollections of what went on behind the scenes for this book, Richard Attenborough issued a statement through his PA saying that 'never having worked with Pat Roc, he was unable to contribute anything useful.'

Most stars would have been put on immediate suspension for three or even six months without pay for such tantrums, but not Pat. Somebody must have been looking after her, probably J. Arthur Rank himself. Instead of suspension, she left with a handsome pay packet containing £1350 [£42,000] for the twelve days of filming she had completed, all of which had to be scrapped. Gilliat was not at all pleased with Pat's departure; it delayed filming for several weeks. But it was mainly his own fault and years later he admitted as much to his friend, Dan Kowalewski, telling him; "I made some serious blunders when I cast *London Belongs to Me*." When production finally restarted, Susan Shaw, a 'graduate' of the Rank Charm School, was drafted in to take Pat's place, not with the top billing which Pat was to have had, but way down the cast list. Susan Shaw, fourteen years Pat's junior, started what looked like being a promising film career in 1946, but following the death of her husband, Bonar Colleano, in 1958, she took to the bottle and died of cirrhosis of the liver in 1978, penniless, the Rank Organisation paying for her funeral.

Richard Attenborough and Louella Parsons, the acerbic American critic admire Pat's Pekingese Floppy on the set of 'London Belongs to Me'. This was before she walked out of the picture.
(Author's Private Collection)

There is no doubt that Pat fell in love easily, and each time was like falling in love for the first time. By the end of 1947, her fickle heart had settled on André Thomas. She couldn't wait to be with him again and, after spending another Christmas with her parents at their home in Bray, and having abandoned Gilliat's film, she was off to Paris for the New Year to meet up with her French lover. Her affair with David MacDonald was now well and truly over. It had run its course and besides, Pat didn't want to get entangled in another messy divorce case.

When Pat returned home, after spending two weeks in Paris with André, it was to an uncertain future with only personal appearances to look forward to. Within days, arrangements were made by Rank for her to travel to Belgium to attend the premiere of Michael Powell and Emeric Pressburger's, *A Matter of Life and Death,* and from there, on to Amsterdam for the premiere of her own film, *Jassy.* Then, back in England, she was sent off to New Brighton for several personal appearances to promote *One Night with You.* "Those early weeks of 1948 were one giddy whirl of travel," wrote Pat in her Fan Magazine.

Regardless of how much she enjoyed meeting her fans, rather naïvely perhaps, Pat couldn't help wondering why the producers in the Rank Organisation weren't casting her in any films. It didn't occur to her that she had labelled herself 'difficult' when she quit *London Belongs to Me* and turned down other roles she deemed unsuitable, including the slapstick comedy, *Cardboard Cavalier,* with Sid Field, one of Britain's most original comedians. Walter Forde, who directed Pat in *The Gaunt Stranger* in 1938, wanted her to play the part of Nell Gwynne, but the 'highfalutin' Patricia Roc was above having custard pies thrown at her in this knockabout film, set in the England of Charles ll. Not so Margaret Lockwood, who begged Forde to cast her, when she heard that Pat wouldn't do it.

No matter how much you dress it up, Pat was becoming impossibly difficult, which inevitably would lead to her eventual downfall. It was something which the British Press picked up on. Leonard Wallace writing in *Picturegoer,* headed his article 'The Riddle of Pat Roc'. In it he wrote;

'From the time she appeared in *The Brothers* her progress halted. Since that picture she has made four others, none of them really bad, none of them distinguished. Just marking time. The mystery is why this ever happened.

It was said that Patricia had been a `difficult` star, a nice nursery term generally used in the film business to cover a multitude of technical misdemeanours like being rebellious about accepting parts which the player considers unsuitable. It was rumoured that some of the producers high up in the Rank group had decided that Pat was getting temperamental, and her refusal to play the part of the typist in *London Belongs to Me* was quite recently put in evidence of that fact.'

In the 3 March 1948 issue of the *Daily Express,* David Lewin wrote much the same sort of thing;

Eighteen months ago Pat was one of the hardest working stars in British pictures, making three pictures at a time. But now she is beginning to realise that she will be 'on holiday' until September or October. There is no new film until then. She has not worked on a picture since she walked out on *London Belongs to Me* four months ago. That was by agreement with the producer – she was not suspended. Maybe Pat was foolish but she thought the part was too dowdy for her.

What Wallace and Lewin neglected to mention of course, was the problem Pat had with Fay Compton on the *London Belongs to Me* set, but perhaps they weren't privy to such sensitive information at the time.

So it was up and down the country, making yet more personal appearance, but at least it kept her in the public eye. One such `task` she performed was judging a cocktail shaking competition at Olympia with radio favourite in the 1940s, Tommy Handley. Another jaunt was an appearance at the Ideal Home Exhibition, where Pat was presented with a new vacuum cleaner, a prize possession in 1948, which she duly gave to her trusted maid and housekeeper Pauline.

She also made a VIP visit to the Wembley Stadium, where Britain was hosting the post war Olympic games, to meet the athletes from the many countries taking part. Her escort was Count Jean de Beaumont, whom she knew well from the days when she used to go skiing in Switzerland before the war. He was a former French Olympian representing his country in the clay pigeon shooting event in 1923, and became of awe-inspiring seniority in the Olympic movement and narrowly missed becoming its president in 1972 when the vote went to his rival Lord Killanin.

The Count and Pat were frequently seen out together during his stay in London and there is little doubt that he spent several passionate evenings at Pat's Hallam Street flat too. Pat's other frequent escort during those summer months was of course, André Thomas. He was in England filming another Terence Young film, *Woman Hater*, at Denham Studios which starred Stewart Granger and French actress Edwige Feuillère.

The French star and Pat were good friends, having met before the war when Pat was anxiously looking for acting parts in France. When they met at the premiere of Edwige's latest French film, *The Eagle Has Two Heads*, at the French Embassy in London, Edwige suggested to Pat that instead of 'marking time' as suggested by Wallace, she should pack her bags and go back to Paris where she was bound to find some film work. This idea particularly appealed to André as it meant that he could keep a watchful eye on the flirtatious Pat. He wasn't without connections in the French film industry, and got in touch with his friend, the French film director Jean Dréville, who secured a small part for Pat in a film he was shortly to co-direct.

Excited at the prospect of working in France and being with André, Pat went to see J. Arthur Rank to ask if she could be released to the French production company Films Marceau, who wanted her in their film *Retour à la Vie.* J. Arthur was very approachable and always ready to listen to his stars' grievances. Sitting at the head of an onyx table which stretched almost the entire length of his office in London's Park Lane, he explained to Pat that there just weren't any films scheduled that would suit her, but promised that as soon as the right story came along she would be the first to know. What he meant to say, but didn't, was that the British producers wouldn't touch her with a barge pole in case she threw a tantrum as she did when making *London Belongs to Me.* He readily agreed that she could spend the summer in Paris if she wanted to. After all, there were only so many 'personal appearances' she could make.

Bags packed, Pat left her London flat in July to play the part of Lieutenant Evelyne in *Retour à la Vie,* a film depicting four different stories about former French prisoners of war returning home after WWII. Pat was in the second segment "Le retour d'Antoine" in which Francois Perrier returns to become a barman in a hotel for American Women's Army Corps (WACs). Although it was only a cameo role, Pat's performance started the critics back in Britain saying again, all the nice things they had hatched up for her when she first hit the screen as a Gainsborough starlet. "Her WACs officer, in one of the light hearted cameos, is Patricia Roc at her best. It took a French film to pull out the real Roc", wrote Francis Koval for *Picturegoer.* "She still isn't the most brilliant player the screen has ever seen, but in *Retour La Vie* she displays an easy, attractive freshness that no one ever discovered when she worked for Mr. Rank." wrote Leonard Mosley in the Daily Express.

The film had its London premiere, attended by Pat, at the Academy Cinema on 20 April 1950. But like many foreign films, it had a limited showing in Britain at the time, even though it was considered good enough to be entered in the 1949 Cannes Film Festival, eventually losing out to Carol Reed's *The Third Man.*

During the making of *Retour à la Vie,* Rank still exercised a certain amount of control over Pat. They assigned her to a five-day whistle-stop visit to Toronto together with her co-star in *So Well Remembered,* Trevor Howard, to represent the Rank Organisation at the opening, on 9 September 1948, of the new 2400-seater Odeon Cinema (later named The Carlton). It was claimed to be the largest cinema in North America at that time, and after all, she was *the goddess of the Odeons*. Quipped Pat during the ceremony; "The theatre is really too good for Canada. We have nothing as good in London and if you don't want it, well, we'll just take it." The cinema was demolished in 1973, the site left derelict for many years.

***

As Pat was finishing her work on *Retour à la Vie*, four actors flew into Orly Airport, Paris, from America. They were there to star in *Man on the Eiffel Tower*, a film about the famous fictional French detective, Inspector Jules Maigret. Their names were Charles Laughton, Franchot Tone, Burgess Meredith and Robert Hutton, the cousin of Woolworth heiress Barbara Hutton. Pat knew them all quite well from her time in Hollywood a couple of years earlier. When she met up with them she told them that she was still at a loose end, with no immediate prospects of film work in Britain. "In that case how would you like a part in *The Man on the Eiffel Tower* I am co-producing with Irving Allen, here in Paris?" Tone asked Pat. She didn't need to think twice about it and jumped at the chance to stay in France a little longer. She was cast as Helen, the wife of Robert Hutton, who was plotting to murder his elderly aunt so that he could collect his inheritance, divorce his wife, and marry his girl-friend Edna, played by Jean Wallace.

Franchot Tone, at one time the husband of Joan +, and at that time, married to Jean Wallace, was a successful actor in the 1930s and early 1940s, who took over producing films that he felt would be challenging and successful. One of his efforts was this psychological B noir film, *The Man on the Eiffel Tower*, based on Georges Simenon's story 'A Battle of Nerves', with Laughton playing Inspector Maigret.

There were various production problems on this picture. For some reason, Laughton didn't get on at all well with the co-producer and director of the film, Irving Allen. After just three days of shooting, Laughton threatened to walk off the picture unless Allen was replaced as director by Meredith. In a huff, Allen stepped down, but he was very dissatisfied with the picture when it was finished. After its initial run in 1949, he bought the film rights back from RKO and kept the prints out of circulation for several years. Many believed that the film was lost forever, even Meredith. But some forty-five years later, after Irving's death in 1987, it was found and released on VHS and DVD.

129

On this occasion, Irving was probably right to pronounce the film 'awful'. But his judgement was not always the best. In the 1950s, he went into partnership with Albert R Broccoli and formed Warwick Films in Britain, but the partnership was strained by their disagreement to bring to the screen the 'James Bond' series. Broccoli was interested, Allen was not. The pair met with Bond author Ian Fleming in 1957 when Allen all but insulted Fleming, declaring that Fleming's novels weren't even *"good enough for television"*.

All these politics did not concern Pat, whose role in the film was very undemanding. Reflecting on the film years later, she had to admit that it was fairly dreadful. "We (Pat and Jean Wallace) were only in the film to add a little glamour to the action and in the end a large amount of our stuff found its way onto the cutting room floor. Our characters were not really important in the story," she said.

By now, her romance with André Thomas had blossomed "If we do get married—and maybe we will — I'll want a quiet wedding. No fuss or bother. The family, friends and fans can wait " Pat told Audrey Whiting of the Daily Mirror on 30 September. But seven days later she dismissed reports that she and André were engaged as 'hooey', probably because André was still legally married to his first wife.

When Rank exercised their right to retain Pat services for a further twelve months, (1 March 1948 to 1 March 1949) they were honour bound by the terms of her contract to pay her the equivalent of fifty filming days at £125 [£3.620] a day, regardless of whether she made any films for them during that period. It therefore made economic sense for Rank to get Pat in front of the cameras before the twelve months were up. It was when she was finishing off her scenes for *Man on the Eiffel Tower*, that she got a call telling her that she had been cast in a sci-fi comedy called *The Perfect Woman*. It was to be produced for Two Cities Films, part of the Rank Organisation, by George and Alfred Black, two of the most famous theatrical impresarios in British light entertainment. This was *fait acomplis*. If Pat had turned down the role she would have been placed on suspension and lost the right to the money. As it was, she reportedly said that she was 'delighted'. After all, it was an opportunity to make her first picture for her employers since completing *One Night With You* over twelve months previously, and an opportunity to be seen again by the British cinema going public. She readily admitted at the time that, whilst her time in Paris with André was heaven, as an actress she hadn't enjoyed the months following the completion of *One Night With You*. She felt as though she had been cast on the scrap heap instead of in films.

John Mills and Pat, dressed as a nurse in a scene from 'So Well Remembered'.
(Author's Private Collection)

Celebrating her thirty-second birthday in 1947, from left: Joan Greenwood, Richard Attenborough, Hazel Court, her sister 'Bobby', David MacDonald, her sister Marie-Louise and Patrick Holt (Courtesy of Michael Thomas)

Pat and her mother dining at the Grosvenor House restaurant with David MacDonald in 1947(Courtesy of Michael Thomas)

Patricia Roc with David MacDonald arriving at the Empire Leicester Square,
May 29 1947, for the premiere of MGM's 'The Yearling' (Author's Private Collection)

*Pat with her parents dining at the Grosvenor House restaurant with
Count Jean de Beaumont in 1948
(Courtesy of Michael Thomas)*

*Pat with Sydney Box arriving at the Gaumont, Haymarket for the premiere of 'When the Bough
Breaks' on November 11, 1947 (Author's Private Collection)*

*Pat, arm-in-arm with her future husband, André Thomas
and Terence Young. Nino Martini, her co-star in 'One Night with You'
is on the right with Floppy leading the way. (Courtesy of Michael Thomas)*

*Christmas in the snow – Pat was never one to shy away from glamour photographs, and the
French magazines loved it! (Author's Private Collection)*

CHAPTER ELEVEN

Marriage No. 2

HER film work in Paris now complete, Pat returned to England, *sans* André Thomas, to prepare for *The Perfect Woman*. But before shooting got under way the following January, there was the annual Royal Command Film Performance to attend on 29 November at the Empire Theatre, Leicester Square. In her fan magazine for December 1948, Pat wrote:

'Just about the time I was due to fly back to England from Paris, the fog clamped down on both sides of the Channel. It was the day before the Command Film Performance and flying was quite out of the question. So I took the boat and arrived in England only a few hours before rehearsal time for the stage show which was put on after *Scott of the Antarctic*. I had a great welcome from all my friends and colleagues – it felt good to be home again.'

One of those colleagues who greeted Pat warmly was none other than Ronald Reagan, eager to renew their intimate relationship. He was in England to make his only British picture *The Hasty Heart* with Richard Todd and Patricia Neal, one time wife of children's author Roald Dahl, and grand-mother of Sophie Dahl. Pat greeted Reagan with open arms as he presented her with an expensive ruby ring.

Describing the Royal occasion, Rank starlet Christine Norden wrote in her unpublished autobiography *The Champagne Days are Over*:

"Shaking with cold and nerves, we all waited to do our little turn on stage. The devastatingly beautiful Patricia Roc, a major box-office star, who was renowned for the number of handsome and famous men who succumbed to her charms, seemed completely at ease, and continued a wild conversation with a horrified Phyllis Calvert, just before we were about to make our entrance. Pat was enthusing over a ruby ring one of her admirers – rumoured to be Ronald Reagan – had just given her. `I love rubies, they are so hot, just like sex`, said Pat.

Although Regan was officially staying at the Savoy Hotel in the Strand, he spent a lot of time at Pat's flat in Hallam Street, where he repeatedly asked her to marry him.

"Ronnie seemed heartbroken and bitterly hurt. His wife told him: 'You're a bore! Get out! I want a divorce.' He was so damaged that often he was drinking and not able to perform sexually," said Pat, adding, "He gave me the most beautiful ruby ring when he proposed marriage. I still have it."

Reagan asked Pat to marry him on more than one occasion, even though Lou Cannon, one of Reagan's many biographers, claimed that he was sceptical about marriage after his painful 1948 divorce from Jane Wyman. "Trouble was," said Pat, "I was in love, or so I thought, with André at that time and had to turn Ronnie down gently."

If the ruby ring was meant to be an engagement ring, Reagan didn't want it back, telling Pat to keep it as a keepsake to remind her of him, and possibly as a sort of 'thank you' for helping him get through his deep depression back in Hollywood when Pat was there filming *Canyon Passage*.

With André working in Paris, the flighty Pat and Reagan continued to spend a lot of time together. But what she may not have known was that when he wasn't seeing her, he was having a relationship with his American co-star, Patricia Neal, who was also staying at The Savoy. Shortly before it was time for him to return home to America, he went to France for three days holiday. Which Pat he took with him however, has never been disclosed, and Patricia Neal was reluctant to discuss the matter when approached years later. However, there is little doubt that Reagan was very much in love with Patricia Roc at the time and she was definitely very fond `the Pres`, as she later in life referred to Reagan, but not enough to want to marry him. That may well have been a lucky escape for Reagan, for had they have made it to the Register Office, and knowing Pat's whimsical reputation, he may well have finished up being twice divorced and permanently distressed. But in any case, as with Charlie Prince, Pat wasn't keen to settle down in America for the rest of her life. Had she have done so, or so she claimed, she would have finished up in the White House as America's First Lady. "I think I would have made a rather good First Lady", she once said. There was just one flaw to that claim; she hadn't read any of the accounts that point out that it was Nancy, Reagan's second wife whom he married in March 1952, who got Ronnie into politics. "Without her, it is very doubtful that he would ever have made it to the White House," said American author George Brandt.

Reagan, born in 1911, spent the majority of his Hollywood career in `B films` where, he joked, the producers "didn`t want them good, they wanted them Thursday". Some considered him to be a poor actor. 'Dull as watching paint dry' was how Doris Day's biographer David Bret described him. But Pat countered that he was a much better actor than people gave him credit for. Arguably he was the most successful actor in history, having catapulted from a career as a Warner Brothers contract player and later television star, into the governorship of California and two terms (1981-1989) as the Republican President of the United States

After he returned home to Hollywood in 1949, Reagan seems to have had little contact with Pat, wasting no time at all before having a string of relationships with fellow actresses. They included Adele Jergens, Penny Edwards - who made a name for herself when she deputised for a pregnant Dale Evans in a number of Roy Rogers films - and Ruth Roman. Then he met the ambitious Nancy Davis.

***

Filming for *The Perfect Woman* under the direction of Bernard Knowles, got under way at Denham Studios in January. Born in 1900, Knowles began his career in 1921 as an assistant cameraman working for Herbert Wilcox. During the 1930s he became associated with director Alfred Hitchcock, filming such thrillers as *39 Steps,* and *Jamaica Inn* before joining Gainsborough Pictures in 1943. He had worked with Pat on two previous occasions; as cinematographer on *Love Story* and later the director on *Jassy.* Pat was looking forward to working with him again.

Based on Wallace Geoffrey and Basil Mitchell's highly successful stage comedy of the same name, *The Perfect Woman* is about Professor Ernest Belmon, a dotty scientist played by Miles Malleson, and his robotic 'perfect woman' invention he has made to resemble his beautiful young niece, Penelope played of course by Pat.

The Professor considers Olga, the name he has given to his robot, to be the perfect woman, a woman who always does as she is told and never answers back. When it is time to test Olga's potential, the Professor engages down-and-out playboy Roger Cavendish and his butler (Nigel Patrick and Stanley Holloway) to take his creation out for the night, and to stay in a honeymoon suite at a posh London hotel. When Penelope, who is fed up with always being cooped up in the house by her over protective uncle, got to hear through her housekeeper, Mrs Butler, played by the glorious Irene Handl, about Olga's intended night out, she decides to take her place and become the robot for a night. The result was utter chaos.

The press book hand-out for the film said that *The Perfect Woman* was warranted to make audiences rock with laughter from beginning to end. Well it hardly did that, but there were moments, particularly when Stanley Holloway and Miles Malleson were on screen, that there was the occasional good laugh.

Pat always enjoyed playing light comedy and, considering her limitations as an actress, put in a delightful performance in this outrageously sexist picture. For some inexplicit reason, Rank's distribution company almost ashamedly kept *The Perfect Woman* out of the West End and didn't give the film the customary showcase of a London première. But her fans, and there were still many, even in 1949, followed her to the suburbs where the film became a big hit. 'The main individual credit for the success of this farce goes to Patricia Roc, whose impersonation of the dummy is perky as the plot demands. Whether parading in a tasteful evening gown or in black lace lingerie she is always *the perfect woman,*' wrote the critic for *Variety*. David Lewin on the other hand wondered why Pat took the part in the first place. "She has almost nothing to do except play at being a robot," he wrote in the *Daily Express*.

If there weren't as many laughs on screen as the producers would have liked, there certainly were off screen. Well, according to Pat there were. "Everyone had one big laugh from beginning to end. Nigel and dear Stanley were a wonderful couple, but they were really mean to me because they tried to make me laugh, never saying the same thing twice running. I was supposed to be a dumb robot and they would constantly try to get me to laugh. That was such fun," she said.

Twenty-one-year-old Pamela Devis, a trained dancer, chosen for the role because it was thought she closely resembled Pat, played Olga the robot. Pamela is now probably better know for the Pamela Devis Dancers she formed, performing throughout the country during the 1960s and 70s, and as resident dance group on ITV's *Sunday Night at the London Palladium*. "Pam tried to teach me a few basic dance steps when we were making the film, but I'm afraid her efforts were wasted. It seems I have two left feet," chuckled Pat.

By now, the writing was on the wall. Pat was no fool and realised that there was no long-term future for her at Rank and that her contract would not be renewed - and she was right. In March, the *London Evening Star* reported, "The latest star to leave the Rank Organisation is Patricia Roc. Her seven-year contract which had a year to run has not been renewed". It went on to say that a Rank official stated, "We hope Miss Roc will continue to make films for us on a freelance basis". She wasn't on her own of course. Many of the stars that the Rank Organisation had created, James Mason, Stewart Granger, Anne Crawford, Valerie Hobson, Phyllis Calvert and Sally Gray for instance, had all vanished from the Rank long-term contract list. Only Margaret Lockwood would stay on a little longer, until 1951 when she asked to be released from her contract, a request Rank unhesitatingly granted.

For a time though, it looked as though Pat's difficult days would be ending. It was widely reported that Herbert Wilcox was going to take her 'under his wing' and had already lined her up for a picture. Knowing how he built up his wife, Anna Neagle, into the country's top female star, Pat's future looked rosy, but nothing further was heard of Wilcox's offer, possibly because Pat had decided to become an exile and make her home in France with André.

Going to France was an astute move on her part. She was now unemployed with no future prospects of film work in Britain, and to cap it all, she owed Rank a considerable amount of money dating back to the time she was inadvertently overpaid living expenses by Universal Studios when she was making *Canyon Passage* in Hollywood. Because the defiant Pat contested the payment, Rank froze the money she earned from *The Perfect Woman*. It would take twelve months before the matter was settled, and not in Pat's favour.

After packing up all her furniture and shipping it out to Paris, she vacated her flat in Hallam Street at the end of March and left England to start a new life in France.

André at the time was busy filming in Paris, so a planned Spring wedding had to be put on hold. In the meantime, Pat settled into her new home, a large Parisian flat, at 88 Boulevard de Courcelles, a stone's throw from the Arc de Triomphe. It took a while to get the flat to her liking, which included installing a huge fireplace, quite unusual in a Parisian house, but once it was finished she was totally 'at home'.

Pat made a brief return visit to London in April to attend the Daily Mail Film Awards at the Dorchester Hotel. That year, Anna Neagle took the female best actress title, unseating Margaret Lockwood who had held the title since 1946.

Pat was placed fifth, which was not bad considering how the Rank Organisation had wilfully neglected her career during the previous two years. Her old flame Michael Wilding took the best actor's award.

When she returned to France after the awards ceremonies, her time was spent following André, who was filming Jean Dréville's *Le Grand Rendez-vous*, on location in Algiers. She had been offered some minor roles in French films but turned them all down, partly to be with her fiancé, but mainly because she was due to start filming that August in Julien Duvivier new picture, *Black Jack*. Duvivier was considered to be one of the greatest figures in the history of French cinema and of world cinema in general. Casting Pat in this smuggling action film was, on paper at least, to be the big break she had been waiting for. Duvivier had signed up André Thomas as lighting cameraman too, so it meant that with *Le Grand Rendez-vous* in the can, there was nothing to stop Pat and André getting married.

Plans were hastily put together for the couple to marry at the town hall in Palaiseau, a small town eleven miles from Paris. André's uncle, Dr. Roger Jardin, the mayor of the town was to perform the civil ceremony. The date was set for 16 August 1949. Both Pat and André wanted a quiet wedding with no fuss. Consequently there were only six people present, which included Pat's sister Marie-Louise, Terence Young, who was their best man, and Jean Dréville. Pat, who carried a huge bouquet of pink roses tied with an Anglo-French ribbon, described her wedding outfit as 'A close fitting hat covered with white feathers, a Paris dress of navy blue silk taffeta with satin spots, and a white muslin fichu'. She looked truly stunning. She never skimped on her appearance, and with her natural elegance everything she wore seemed perfect.

CHAPTER TWELVE

Filming Without Pay

THE newlyweds left Paris for Majorca two days after their marriage, not on honeymoon, although it must have seemed like it, but to start filming *Black Jack*. The shooting schedule was set for eight weeks but it would be almost seven months before it was finished. The film started out with the title *Man from Jamaica* and was to star American actor Louis Hayward. That pleased Pat. Speaking with a distinct American accent, Pat explained to David Lewin what she felt was wrong with her British Pictures. "I never had real leading men. They weren't romantic enough. I wanted someone who was a big figure in films. But when I had John Mills, he was playing an old man. In my next picture I have Louis Hayward to play opposite me. That will help to make it good," she told him. However, the title changed to *Black Jack*, and much to Pat's disappointment, so did her leading man. When Hayward learnt that there was to be no contractual salary for the principal actors, which included Pat, he refused to have anything to do with the picture and George Sanders was hastily drafted in to replace him. The deal was that the principal actors would only receive travel and living expenses during the production. Their salary was to be paid out of the picture's box office receipts. But as *Black Jack* was a flop and lost money, nobody got paid. In Pat's autograph book, Sanders wrote "We have to 'keep on fighting' until we get paid!

Produced, written as well as directed by Duvivier, the film, described by the *New York Times* as a 'trashy and absurd little melodrama' is about a notorious drug smuggler known as Captain Black Jack (George Sanders), who falls in love with an East European refugee, played by Pat, and gets killed for his troubles. Also in this complex intertwining story is Agnes Moorehead, who turns out to be not the eccentric, silliest lady on the island, but a rival drug racketeer, and Herbert Marshall, a solicitous doctor, who in reality is an undercover agent tracking down Sanders.

Although effectively directed by Duvivier in many scenes, particularly the sequence involving a mysterious dramatic search in the Majorcan caves, and strikingly photographed by André Thomas (although some of his close ups of his bride were anything but flattering) the film was totally ruined by Margarita de Ochoa's editing. In the climax of the film, for instance, the action on the two boats is so badly edited that it is very difficult to work out exactly what is going on. The screenplay was also very poor, and both Pat and Sanders complained daily about the Americanized dialogue. Sanders got so fed up with the entire project that he hid himself away whenever he could with his bride of four months, Zsa Zsa Gabor, spending his time eating and sleeping, with the result that he put on a lot of weight during the long months of production. The change is apparent in the film: scenes shot early in the schedule show him quite fit but in later ones he appears noticeably heavier. Pat, on the other hand, spent her free time, and there was a lot of that, swimming and riding. She was not one to let herself go!

In spite of the all the production difficulties, Pat had a lot of fun making the picture, even though, as much as she liked George Sanders, she was not too keen on working with him. "He never looked at you," said Pat. "In a scene that is intimate, you usually look at the person, but he would either look at my forehead, or look at my nose. He couldn't or wouldn't look me in the eyes. It was quite difficult working with him. He could be quite a moody person too; he was a Russian and had a bit of a temper. Funnily enough it was much like that with Maxwell Reed when we were making *The Brothers*, the difference being however, Max didn't have George's talent."

Back home from Majorca, Madame Thomas, as she now was, and her husband settled down to a little quiet home life together, and in Pat's case, hoping that a baby would put in an appearance. She would have to wait a further two years for that to happen. But at least she was content, telling journalist Francis Koval in June 1950 that she felt happier than she had ever felt before.

Her initial decision to quit Britain required a certain amount of courage. She presumably still had some sort of a career and a future in the British film industry. She could even have made a name for herself in television too, as Phyllis Calvert and Ann Crawford had done around about that time. But for some time she had been unhappy with the direction of her career and felt that she could do better in France. In many respects it seems that marrying André, a prominent figure in the French film industry was a means to an end. Her well-meaning friends thought that she was mad to go, and that she sacrificing everything for love, but she didn't see it that way. Whilst pursuing a career in France, she hoped, with the help of Eric Goodhead her agent who she still retained, that it would be possible to hop over the Channel at least once a year to make a film in Britain. Her hopes were raised when Terence Young visited Pat and André in Paris. He promised to put her in his next film, but that, like Herbert Wilcox's interest in her, came to nothing. She did eventually get two decent film parts in England, as we shall see later, but by now the British studios were counting on a new generation of stars, stars like Diana Dors, Virginia McKenna, and Sylvia Syms. The female stars of the 1940s on whom the film industry had relied during the turbulent war years, were no longer in demand. Gone were the 'women's pictures', to be replaced by a spate of war films with virtually all male casts. Apart from that, the masses who queued up weekly in the 1940s to see a film, no matter how bad it was, were turning away from the cinema for the comforts of their own home – and television

Pat's next picture was a co-production between the feisty young Quebec Films in Canada and the old established Eclectiques Films of Paris. Called *Son Copain*, (retitled *L'Inconnue de Montréal* in Canada) with a budget of almost 200,000 Canadian dollars, filming got under way in June 1950 under the direction of Jean Devaivre. Pat plays a suspected murderess called Helen, an unusual character for her, who is being pursued by the Royal Canadian Mountie, Paul Dupuis. She is sheltered by her fiancé Pierre played by French favorite René Dary. A lot of the film was shot on location in Canada, which Pat enjoyed. "The film was good in its own way. At least I thought it was, though I don't think you'll find it anywhere. It was one of the more obscure films that didn't get to England. But it was quite successful in Canada I believe," said Pat.

The French way of life suited Pat. "I really enjoy, even prefer, working in France," she said. "Back in England I would tumble out of bed at five-thirty in the morning to be ready made-up and on the film set at Denham by nine o'clock. Whereas in France, we seldom start before mid-day, then we work right through the afternoon and evening without a break. Then at about 7.30pm aperitifs are served on the set, which is a far more civilised way of doing things." On the face of it, it seemed that Pat had found a recipe for living which suited her perfectly. Not only that, but all Paris was talking about Patricia Roc as one of the strongest screen personalities they had encountered for a long time. Hardly a week went by without her being seen in some French magazine or other, and both she and André were always in demand to attend film premières and private parties. At this stage in her life, Pat was noticeably more assured and enthusiastic for both her work and life in general. Leonard Mosley of the *Daily Express*, who bizarrely   once said of Pat that 'she looked like a strapping, healthy girl who provoked about as much palpitation as a newt' attributed her transformation to André Thomas, her husband, who, able to exploit her talents more fully, could take credit for the way in which Pat projected herself on the screen. A means to an end, indeed!

On a late Autumn afternoon, Pat was busy tidying her Parisian flat eagerly awaiting the arrival of Jacques Tourneur, the Frenchman who directed her in *Canyon Passage* five years earlier. Remembering her delicate performance in that film, he wanted her to play the female lead in *Circle of Danger*, a film he was about to start shooting in England. He talked persuasively, and Pat wanting to fulfil her ambition to make at least one picture a year in Britain, happily and eagerly signed a one picture contract. She was even more excited when told that Ray Milland, best known for his Oscar winning portrayal of an alcoholic writer in Billy Wilder's *The Lost Weekend*, was going to be her leading man. Born in Wales, Milland was eight years older than Pat, suave, sophisticated and an inveterate seducer of attractive actresses. "You had to run past Ray Milland's dressing room or else," remembered actress Patricia Medina, whose was married to *Robin Hood* actor Richard Greene and later to Joseph Cotton.

Pat wasn't the type to run past anybody's dressing room, especially if the occupant was Ray Milland, the man whom Tony Curtis referred to as 'poison'. Whether she ever went in is not known, but it is hard to believe that Milland didn't test his luck, not that he would have boasted had he succeeded. He was always the height of discretion and even more so when he was filming *Circle of Danger*, having brought his wife Muriel – known to friends as 'Mal' - with him to England. She was accustomed to rumours about her husband and may well have heard about Pat's penchant for other women's husbands. It seems she had little to worry about on this occasion, but not so two years later when her husband fell hopelessly in love, during the filming of Alfred Hitchcock's *Dial M for Murder*, with Grace Kelly who, according to Hedy Lamarr, would sleep with anyone in Hollywood, actors, producers, directors, in order to get ahead in the business.

Circle of Danger, based on the book *White Heather* by Philip MacDonald, was filmed on location in Wales and Devon and at Worton Hall Studios in

Isleworth, the studio where Humphrey Bogart and Katharine Hepburn filmed scenes for John Huston's *The African Queen* that same year. The story revolves around an American, played by Milland, who comes to Britain to hunt out six people who can help him get to the bottom of the mystery surrounding his younger brother's death during a Commando raid on St. Celeste in France in 1940. Early in the story he meets Elspeth , Pat's character, and they fall in love. It was a part that Pat enjoyed playing and offered her just the kind of opportunity she lacked in her earlier British pictures. Her character is real. It has vitality and plays a prominent part in a tightly written script. Tourneur assembled an experienced and talented supporting cast. Hugh Sinclair is a Scots ex-army officer and friend of Elspeth, a writer and illustrator of children's books; Marius Goring is a sinister gay ballet dancer; Naunton Wayne is a convincing East End used car salesman. His girlfriend Bubbles is played by Dora Bryan. This is not an action packed film, but one in which Tourneur concentrates on a series of character studies of the remaining Commandos who Milland relentlessly pursues and quizzes. As for Ray Milland and Pat, their performance together is somewhat reminiscent of Dick Powell and Myrna Loy of *The Thin Man* series, where the couple flirt and banter wittily as they solve crimes with relative ease.

When the film was released on 21 May 1951, fan magazine *Picture Show* said of it: "The sincerity of the acting, clever characterisation and deft direction lift this film well above the usual mystery melodrama," whilst *Variety*, on its release in the States, said of Pat: "Her role is not too demanding from a thespic standpoint but she fits the picture's pulchritude needs." At the end of the film, after a series if tiffs, Pat asks Milland for a lift home. "Going a long way," he growled. "I don't mind how far it is," she said, and his eyes light up, as well they might. Not having seen her on the screen for some time, the British audience fell in love with Patricia Roc all over again.

During the making of *Circle of Danger*, Pat stayed with her sister in Bray and flew back to Paris for long weekends whenever the filming schedule allowed, which wasn't that often. This arrangement didn't suit André, who became increasingly resentful about her continuing absence. It wasn't the sort of marriage he had bargained for, and it was to a sullen husband whenever she managed to return home. Inevitably, cracks began to appear in the marriage.

CHAPTER THIRTEEN

A Baby at Last

IT was whilst Pat was enjoying the success of *Circle of Danger* that she got the devastating news that her mother was dangerously ill. Muriel Riese had suffered a cerebral haemorrhage that had left her brain damaged and in a semi coma from which she never recovered. She was admitted to Wyke House in Isleworth, a private mental home run by Dr. G.W. Smith, O.B.E. "The whole family was distraught," recalled Bobby, Pat's sister. "It was totally unexpected, although the doctor had said that mum had been living with 'a time bomb' waiting to go off at any time, ever since the day she had been thrown out of a taxi, severely hitting her head on the road, when it was involved in an accident in Park Lane during the war." Muriel died 8 October 1951 in Wyke House. Her age was given as 54 although this did not tally precisely with other official documents, which showed her to be at least three years older.

It was a sad occasion for Pat the day Muriel was buried at the Hanwell Cemetery on a damp misty day in October. Both she and André attended the funeral, along with many family friends. Pat had always been close to her mother, although she rarely spoke about her in public. As she watched the coffin lowered into the grave she became even more conscious that she was still waiting for the baby she so desperately wanted, and that she hadn't provided a grandchild for her mother.

After the funeral, André returned home leaving Pat with her family. She needed to spend some time with her father and sister Marie-Louise, a need which didn't go down at all well with André.

The couple were now spending a lot of their time with their three dogs at the spacious farmhouse in Vallangoujard, a small village on the outskirts of Paris, which they shared with their close friend Jean Dréville. Each dog had its own colour matching lead, collar and dog bowl and were described by André's aunt as 'uneducated', inferring that they were, to a degree, spoilt. André Thomas

147

was not best pleased to be on his own again with the dogs, although he had the comfort of having Dréville to share his concerns about his failing marriage.

The Thomases managed to hide their domestic troubles from the cinematic world and fans; to all intents and purposes they seemed content with their lives. But it became obvious to André's close family that behind closed doors, the tension built. "*Il est devenu évident que la situation à la maison s'est détériorée à partir de 1951 à la suite de difficultés matérielles rencontées par le ménage,*" said Patrick Jardin, André's nephew. It was as if André expected Pat to stay at home and play the welcoming wife when he got in from filming, instead of gallivanting across the Channel for months at a time to make films in England. Pat was normally one of the easiest people in the world to get along with, but she drew the line when it came to possessive husbands. Murray Laing tried it and failed, and now it seemed that André was making the same mistake. Freedom to make her own decisions was something Pat had always cherished, and she wasn't about to capitulate now.

After the death of her mother, Pat spent several weeks in England during which time she went to see Eric Goodhead and pleaded with him to find her a decent role in a British picture, which he did. Rank at the time was promoting their latest protégé, Anthony Steel. They wanted to try him in a light comedy picture to see how he faired, and Pat seemed the perfect choice to play his wife in *Something Money Can't Buy*, a post-war comedy about the problems facing army personnel adjusting to life in civvy street after being demobbed.

Pat returned to Paris well in time for Christmas. It may have been cold outside in the streets, but in Pat and André's flat the atmosphere was definitely frosty, especially when she announced to her sombre husband that in the new year, she would be away filming in England, for several weeks.

It was almost four years since she made *Perfect Woman*, her last film for Rank, so she was 'over the moon' to be back making a picture for the British cinema mogul again. And the British press were glad to see her back. *Picturegoer* summed it up nicely:

> "Pat Roc comes back to Britain with that special line of oomph that's at a very low ebb in our studios".
> "What's Pat Roc got that the others are short of? Plenty. Let's say she's the shot in the arm that the romantic side of British film-making is crying out for. We've plenty of nice young things who can put a neat profile in front of the camera. But we're woefully short on the Jane Russell element".

Quite an accolade, although Pat could hardly be compared to Jane Russell. Miss Russell was a lady who personified the sensuously contoured sweater girl look, which certainly wasn't Pat's style. But perhaps the two actresses did have one thing in common, and that was displaying *mucho* cleavage – Jane in the western *The Outlaw,* and Pat in *The Wicked Lady.*

It was claimed that Paris had given Pat a French accent and mannerisms to match. Waving her hands, she reportedly said at the pre-production press conference for *Something Money Can't Buy* in February 1952, "I am so *appEE* I am back. I like making British pictures". But beneath the bubbling surface there was an air of sadness. Ever since she had married André, she had been hoping for a baby. "It's all we long for in life, but so far we have been unlucky", she told the *Daily Mirror* reporter, adding, "We have drawers full of baby clothes at home, most of which I have knitted and we are still hoping." André Thomas had already fathered a daughter with his first wife so there shouldn't have been a problem doing the same for Pat. However, it had now been acknowledged by the couple, that for whatever reason, André was the one who had difficulty in getting Pat pregnant. Yet she continued to insist that she and her husband were still trying for a baby. Then, in July of that year, Pat triumphantly announced that she was pregnant. "Most people probably don`t see me as the type of girl who is longing to be a mother, but from my early twenties it has been my greatest wish. But then it took so long to find the perfect husband and even now we've had to wait four years," Pat told the press with conviction. But the baby wasn't André's, the 'perfect husband' who she was beginning to despise. So who was the father? The answer was Anthony Steel.

Anthony Steel, one of the highest paid British actors during the 1950s was tall, handsome, well connected, and gentlemanly on screen, if not always off it. Pat and Steel were comparative strangers, never having worked together before, or come to that, met up socially. But following their introductions they wasted little time before secretly embarking on a very passionate love affair off screen. Not even the crew were aware of it. "I had no idea that it was whilst working on *Something Money Can't Buy* that Pat became pregnant by Tony," said Julie Harris, the Oscar winning costume designer, who designed Pat's fabulous dresses for the film. "We all knew that they got on well together, but not to that extent."

One person who was in on their secret was Steel's friend, actor Michael Trubshawe who played one of Steel's army chums in the film. Trubshawe, a massive 6ft 6ins tall ex-army officer with a huge handlebar moustache and an eccentric talent for getting into trouble, owned a small residential club, The Old Ship at Bosham in West Sussex. Typical of the man, he gave Tony and Pat a year's free membership, so that they could act out their clandestine affair away from any prying eyes. Given their celebrity status and the spotlight in which they both lived, it must have been difficult for them to disguise their romantic friendship. Fortunately, the intrusiveness of the press had not really reached the proportions that it has nowadays, but even so, there would still have been an overwhelming need for secrecy. A whiff of any scandal would have had serious consequences for Steel's career had either Arthur Rank or John Davis found out about their contract star's affair, especially as both he, although separated, and Pat were married at the time.

Anthony Steel was five years younger than Pat and had served as an officer during the Second World War. After the war, and a bit of stage acting, he was offered a seven year contract with Rank.

For the first couple of years he was groomed for stardom playing small roles, most of them uncredited, in a handful of 'B' films. His major opportunity came in 1950 when he was cast as one of the officers who devised a novel method of escaping from a German prisoner-of-war camp. The film was *The Wooden Horse*, and established him as a star personality.

Something Money Can't Buy was an important step in the development of Steel's career, and aimed at showing him as much at home in the drawing-room romantic comedy as he was in the stirring intensities of a prison camp. Pat was billed ahead of Steel, but her part was little more than a foil for him. Nevertheless, and not surprisingly, there was a certain chemistry between them that showed up on the screen. "The screen discovers a new romantic team, they are terrific together" read the film's publicity posters. In fact it was whispered that the two of them could star in a sequel. It was during filming that Pat said; "I feel that Anthony and I are really settling down to 'married life' in the first British family comedy for some years. Certainly it would make me happy if *Something Money Can't Buy* proved to be the starting point for a whole series of films with us in them."

It didn't of course. Although there was a good supporting cast; A. E. Matthews, Moira Lister, Diane Hart, and David Hutcheson, the film falls short on many fronts. The script by Pat Jackson, who also directed the film, and James Lansdale Hodson was clumsy in both characterisation and its picture of English society. Instead of genuine laughs from the audience, there were merely a few chuckles. Leslie Halliwell thought the film was; "A weakly contrived comedy, which makes nothing of its possibilities and is limply handled all round." Then there was the *Monthly Film Bulletin's* verdict; "Whilst Anthony Steel plays competently as Harry, Patricia Roc is charmless as his wife."

Oh dear! What did Pat have to do to win over the critics, or didn't she really care? The answer is that she probably didn't care. By the time the film went on general release in August, much to her delight, she was five months pregnant with the baby she had always wanted. "I do want to be sure the baby is born in England," she said, and promptly made her reservation in a London nursing home for some time in December.

It is almost certain that Pat made a conscious decision to get herself pregnant by Steel before she even left Paris to start work on the film. She was rapidly approaching her thirty-seventh birthday and her body clock was telling her that time was running out if she was to have that baby she so much craved. She had called time on André a long time ago, and threw caution to the wind after she met Steel. Interviewed by Michael Thornton in 1995, he asked her what had drawn her to him. She laughed and said simply, "Animal magnetism. I'm afraid he was very, very good in bed. Also, I desperately wanted a child by that point, and I had fallen utterly and completely out of love with André. I saw my affair with Tony as the last chance I might have to become a mother, so I grabbed it."

There is no doubt that Steel was fully aware of Pat's motive and willingly offered his services - *all in the cause of duty* – and who could blame him. His one proviso of course, was that he didn't want anything to do with the baby, financially or otherwise - and he didn't. Pat obviously had genuine feelings for Anthony Steel, describing him as 'as the love of my life'. But once the filming for *Something Money Can't Buy* was over, there was to be no happy ending as there was in the film. They both went their separate ways and didn't meet up again for several years.

Steel was married to top London fashion model Juanita Forbes at the time, but had walked out on her in 1950 when he realised that he was going to be a big star. They divorced in 1954. Two years later he met and married the much talked about blonde Swedish actress Anita Ekberg. "Anita is the most beautiful woman I have ever met," he declared. Their marriage lasted barely three years.

Nobody seems to know whether Pat confessed to André, when she returned to Paris, that she was pregnant and the baby wasn't his. However, whatever was said between the two of them in their Paris apartment, and remember, the marriage was now in terminal decline, André seemed overjoyed at the news. His godson, Prosper Jardin is convinced that André genuinely thought he was the father. "He seemed so pleased and the family was so excited when we heard the news," he said.

Whilst Pat was waiting to have her baby, that summer she was offered a leading role by writer-director Giuseppe Masini to appear in his film, *La mia vita é tua* (My Life is Yours). Her co-star was Armando Francioli, an Italian actor who became a favourite in his own country through regular appearances on television in the 1960s and 1970s. Because she couldn't speak good enough Italian, she made the film in English and her voice was dubbed. *La mia vita é tua*, a romantic story about Francioli's choice of beautiful women, hence Pat's casting, did reasonable well in Italy, but it was never shown in Britain.

The film was made at Cinecittà, the large film studio in Rome that many considered the hub of the Italian cinema. This was the opportunity Pat was looking for, the chance to get away from Paris and André for a while. She rented a small apartment and set up home in the capital for the seven weeks it took to make the film. Whilst she was there, she had frequent visits from André's family. As far as they were concerned, André and Pat were going to have a baby, still totally in the dark about the true circumstances of her pregnancy. Even as late as 2009, some members of the family still had no idea, even though years earlier, Yannick Thomas, André's daughter, had blurted out one day that Michael Thomas, Pat's son was not her brother. According to Patrick Jardin, the family totally dismissed her allegations, which they thought were said out of spite, because she was resentful towards Pat, blaming her for the break-up of her parent's marriage.

When *La mia vita é tua* was completed, Pat travelled back to Paris to prepare for the birth of her baby. It was Dr. Roger Jardin, an obstetrician and André's uncle who had officiated at Pat and André's wedding, who brought André Michel (which Pat later changed to Michael Alan) into the world on 12 December 1952, not in England, as Pat had hoped, but in France. Just as she was preparing to travel to England for the birth, dense fog lasting several days brought London to a standstill. It was so bad that at Sadler's Wells, a performance of *La Traviata* was stopped when the audience could no longer see the stage, the fog having infiltrated the theatre. The atrocious conditions led to widespread disruption of rail, road and air travel and put paid to Pat leaving Paris.

There was a constant stream of visitors from André's family whilst she was in the Palaiseau clinic, none more so than 'the proud father'. He still showed no signs of acknowledging that it was not him but another man who was the father of Pat's baby. To all intense and purpose it was his child, and now that Pat had got the baby she had been longing for, he was convinced that their marital difficulties would be resolved. It was however too late for that. Pat had fallen out of love with him and the couple grew further and further apart. Perhaps unwisely, André negotiated a directing assignment in India for six months, to work on the Bollywood production, *Mayurpankh*. Whether he thought a trial separation would be the answer, we don't know, but if he did, it didn't work, well not for Pat it didn't. After three years of marriage, she really couldn't have cared less if she never saw him again.

During his prolonged absence, Pat remained good friends with his family, staying with them on occasions during the months immediately after Michael was born at the family home in Amanlis. They were well aware that Pat and André were going through a rough patch, but they didn't take sides. Perhaps they would have, had they known who Michael's father really was, but that secret was known to but a few. "Pat had two lives and she never mixed the two," said her sister Bobby. "There was her working life which became very public when she was at the top. Then there was her private life, which boy! did she keep to herself. Even I didn't know who Michael's real father was until many, many years later, and I don't think any of our family knew either."

When Michael was eight months old, Pat felt it was safe to return to work. She was offered another leading role in an Italian production, and in August 1953 went off to Rome to film *Cartouche*. Directed by Hungarian Steve Sekely, the story is about Jacques de Maudy, an eighteenth-century French nobleman accused of murder. He adopts the name Cartouche to hide his true identity and flees to Italy where he joins a troupe of strolling players. There, he meets and falls in love with Donna Violante, played by Patricia Roc. She helps him, and with Donna at his side, he returns honourably to his estates in France. It's a film that bears all the hallmarks of *Scaramouche* filmed two years earlier with Stewart Granger in the leading role.

Cartouche was played by American actor Richard Basehart. Whilst he never really took Hollywood by storm, he was always kept busy, his best performances being in the gritty film-noir classic *He Walked by Night*, and Federico Fellini's 1954 poignant masterpiece *La Strada*. His last acting job was providing the narration at the closing ceremony of the Summer Olympic

Games in Los Angeles in 1984. The following day he suffered the first of a series of strokes and died four weeks later. Pat found him a gentle likeable man to work with and like her, a true animal lover. Together with his third wife Diana, and supported by Doris Day, he founded the 'Actors and Others for Animals', a charity which was dedicated to the promotion of the humane treatment of animals.

When *Cartouche* was released in Britain in February 1956, it was the first time Pat had been seen on the British cinema screen since the release of *Something Money Can't Buy* in the summer of 1952. Clearly, she found a place in the heart of the trade paper *Daily Film Renter's* critic reviewing *Cartouche*. 'How pleasant it is to see Patricia Roc back again after too long an absence, although, it is not as if she has a great deal to do other than look her attractive self,' he wrote.

During the making of the film, André Thomas travelled to Rome to see Pat and 'his' son Michael. He had no work commitments there, so it can only be assumed that he wanted to try and give the marriage one more chance. If this was the case it didn't work out the way he had hoped. During an almighty row between the couple, at last, André accused Pat of committing adultery and claimed that Michael was not his. But even then, he still wanted Michael to be thought of as 'his son'. He hoped that in time he and Pat could reconcile their differences and return to the loving relationship they had had when they first married. He was besotted by Pat and genuinely loved Michael, even though he knew in his heart that he was not the true father.

But for Pat, it was all too late. At a press conference in February 1955, she told the assembled journalists that she no longer liked or loved André. In the *Daily Herald* she is quoted as saying: "Stars usually blame the fact that they are kept apart by their work. With André and me it wasn't only that. After a time, I found I simply didn't like him anymore." In the *Daily Mail* she also made it clear how she felt: "You spend months apart because your work cannot keep you together and when you meet again, well you find the old spark has gone. The plain truth is that I don't love him anymore."

Why was Pat so vehement towards André, what had he done that was so terrible? He was after all, according to his family, a gentle and kind man, not prone to tantrums, and known as 'Uncle Lamb' by his young nephew Patrick because of his soft nature and his curly hair. Maybe it was because Pat now resented living in Paris and blamed André for her no longer being a box-office name in Britain. "My time in Europe has taught me to be more sophisticated, but I have lost more than I have gained by going," she told a *Daily Herald* journalist.

When André read that Pat no longer 'liked' or 'loved' him, he was emotionally hurt. He didn't take kindly to Pat's outburst and within three weeks applied to the Parisian courts for Michael to be returned to Paris and the marital home. Pat was now staying with her sister, Marie-Louise, and had no intention of ever returning to Paris to live. She immediately consulted her solicitor, and on 21 April petitioned for a divorce. She was playing a very dangerous game. Had the petition gone to court the whole saga of her infidelity with Anthony Steel would unquestionably have come out into the open. As it was, she was spared that embarrassment. Whether it was stress caused by the whole sorry situation, or perhaps the pressure of work, possibly the combination of the two, André suffered a massive stroke early in 1956, whilst he was making *Le Sang à la Tête* on location at La Rochelle, the seaport in south western France. His health deteriorated rapidly and, complicated by a kidney disease, he died on 22 November that year. He was 45.

Pat was now a free woman, but not in the circumstances she would have wished. André Thomas was buried on 24 November at Vallangoujard, the village where the couple had spent many fun hours during happier times. Pat was at the graveside to say her goodbyes. She may even have shed a few tears for the man she thought she loved back in 1949, which in effect, just about sums Pat up; a warm, vital, outgoing woman who was always in love with *being in love*, even though on occasions it was only temporarily.

CHAPTER FOURTEEN

The Widow

THE last time André saw Michael Thomas was in March 1954. That was when Pat left Rome to go to Turin to make yet another Italian picture, a picture that turned out to be one of her all-time favourites. Called *The Widow (La Vedova X* in Italy). Pat's co-star was Massimo Serato playing a racing driver who falls in love with Pat's character, a rich, attractive widow who is supposed to be quite a bit older than him. In reality Serato was only eleven months younger than Pat. He later meets and falls in love with a much younger girl, Anna Maria Ferrero, who in turn falls in love with a younger racing driver played by Leonardo Botta. Quite a love tangle and triangle, resolved when Anna Maria marries her younger racing driver, and Serato is killed in a motor race, leaving Pat alone with just her memories.

This was the second consecutive picture Pat had made with Massimo Serato – he played Henri de Vauboranche, the villain in *Cartouche.* They got on well together, but whilst they shared several dinner dates, there has never been any suggestion of romantic liaison. Pat had to tread very carefully not to be seen as an unsuitable mother for fear of losing Michael to André, who she felt was watching her every move. She was advised to steer clear of any intimate relationships at that time.

"With Patricia Roc as attractive as ever, and the Lewis Milestone's touch well apparent in direction and story, the presentation of a rich widow's emotional troubles is strong faire, well acted by an international cast," was the verdict of the *Monthly Film Bulletin* when *The Widow* was eventually released in Britain in 1962. It was in fact a somewhat curious film from Milestone, veering from women's magazine format, to a stylish and cynical study of a triangular affair.

Pat loved making *The Widow.* "It was an absolutely terrific film and for that we must thank, of course, Lewis Milestone. He was a very talented and experienced director," she said. Milestone's niche in film history is secure with his two Academy Awards. He was the very first recipient of the best director's

Oscar in 1929 for his comedy, *Two Arabian Knights,* and was awarded a second in 1930 for *All Quiet on the Western Front,* a harrowing screen adaptation of the antiwar novel by Erich Paul Remarque, whose widow, Hollywood star Paulette Goddard, was to become a good friend of Pat in later life.

The Widow was the sort of film that gave Pat the opportunity to cast off that 'namby-pamby' role, which she maintained, had plagued her since her Gainsborough days. "I am not an ingénue any more, today I am now a mature woman," Pat told Joseph Garrity, who was interviewing her for *TV Times* in 1956. "My part in *The Widow,* my last continental picture, was right up my street. I play the role of a ruthless, scheming cynical woman in love with a man ten years younger – a woman determined to get what she wants by fair means or foul. It's the kind of role that Joan Crawford or Bette Davis would play, which now suits me best; the kind of role that I want in British films and I am content to wait for it." That part, sadly, never materialised for Pat. Eric Goodhead, her agent, did what he could, but for a fading star, the best he could come up with was a handful of guest appearances in the television series of the day, and some very mediocre low budget 'B' pictures. Oh, how she must have longed for the roles she snubbed her nose up in the past! But now she was on her own and work, no matter what, was a necessity. Asked by journalist Denise Robins for *She Magazine* in June 1955 whether a woman should put her career or her child first, Pat, whose son Michael was now two-and-a-half years old, replied, somewhat diplomatically:

"It is obvious that I share this problem with thousands of career women throughout the world. One should judge it not selfishly but in relation to the child's future. Obviously, if any mother works it is not usually for the pleasure of it, but for economic and social reasons.
If I am fortunate enough to be able to provide my son – through my work – with the extra little touches and the extra education which will better fit him to face the future on his own, then I am not only entitled but duty bound to continue my career, and let a good nurse or relative take care of him when I am not around."

By now Pat, was yesterday's film star and on her way to becoming just a symbol of silver screen nostalgia. Between 1950 and 1962, as most of the female movie stars of Patricia Roc`s age were being put out to pasture, her choices grew less and less and in spite of her protestations about only accepting roles where `the character must be strong` she more or less took what she could get, which invariably was not that good. "If I have a jinx," she said at the time, "then a few others must have one too. Margaret Lockwood, Ann Todd and Jean Kent are just a few who have had little or no work in films. I am disappointed but not worried about this waiting. Joan Crawford, remember, was out of films for six years. Now she's at the top again. I have a feeling that just around the corner something will turn up for me," she added. There was one offer that she reportedly turned down – perhaps unwisely; that was in the film *Now and Forever,* playing mother to Thora Hird's eighteen-year old daughter Janette Scott who, as a baby, was in one of Pat's Gainsborough successes, *2000 Women.*

"Maybe I left it too late to make a comeback in Britain. The whole nature of films seemed to have changed whilst I was away," Pat said when reflecting on her cinematic demise. So, putting aside any thoughts of playing 'a real woman' as she had done in *The Widow,* Pat was now prepared to accept anything (except mothers to glamorous eighteen-year-olds apparently) if only to be seen again on the screen, and to remind people that she was still around. With that in mind, Pat accepted one of the leading roles in *The Hypnotist,* a film produced by Anglo Amalgamated Productions. This was a small British film production company run by Nat Cohen and Stuart Levy, whose output was mainly low budget and often second feature films. *The Hypnotist* fell neatly into that category - a typical 1950s run of the mill low budget thriller, with so many unconnected subplots that it became hopelessly confusing. Val Neal, played by Canadian ice hockey player and one time crooner with the Ted Heath band, Paul Carpenter, is a pilot who is injured when a plane he is testing crashes. From then on he suffers blackouts. When his fiancée Mary (Pat's character) is informed that his illness is psychosomatic, she replies: "What does that mean?" She then suggests that her uncle, Francis Pelham, a psychiatrist and hypnotist, might be able to help. This is the perfect opportunity for Pelham, played by Roland Culver, to do away with his wife. Placing Val Neal under hypnosis, Pelham orders him to kill his wife. When Neal fails, the doctor murders his wife himself and attempts to frame Neal. This is where Pat, looking just as glamorous as ever and well belying her forty-one years, comes to the rescue as the devoted fiancée. Through her investigations she reveals the gruesome truth and proves Neal's innocence. Not a very good film, and certainly not one that was going to get her back in the mainstream of pictures. She would have done far better if she had accepted the role in *Now and Forever,* which award-winning actress Pamela Brown, who spent her last days living with Michael Powell, gladly accepted.

For some strange reason when the *Hypnotist* went over to America, it was re-titled *Scotland Yard Dragnet:* a bit of an oxymoron as it features neither a police dragnet nor, till the final part of the film, someone from Scotland Yard. That 'someone' was of course William Hartnell, whose career was defined by mainly playing policemen and soldiers. The following year he starred in the first of the thirty-one *Carry On* films, but is probably best remembered now for playing the first Dr. Who in 1963.

There appeared to have been a stigma in being branded a 'TV actor' in Britain back in the 1950s. It was as if there was some kind of snobbery about being a film actor versus a television actor. But when yesterday's stars were no longer being offered work and the public that once adored them were fast forgetting they still existed, they would turn to television if it became available to them. It was almost that, if you wanted to work, then television was the only outlet. Phyllis Calvert, from the mid-1950s on, was regularly seen on TV right up until two years before her death in 2002. Among her credits was that of Kate, an agony aunt, in thirty-eight episodes of the series of the same name. Margaret Lockwood also finished her career appearing in television productions, including *Justice* during the 1970s. She played the part of a female barrister, Harriet Peterson, in the long running series.

Pat remembered what Noel Coward had told her several years earlier; "Never turn a job down, no matter how small it is, because if you are not working, you are not acting." She turned to television because, now living in an elegant apartment, 77 Dorset House in Gloucester Place, just off Baker Street, with her son, she still had to pay the bills and sustain a reasonable lifestyle befitting a 'star' - a lifestyle that could work out to be quite costly. For instance, whilst she owned many cars during her life, she never learnt to drive which meant that wherever she went, it was always by taxi or private car, and that could be expensive.

Her first role in a television production was in the *Errol Flynn Theatre* series, (re-titled *Mystery Adventure* for the American market). Flynn came to England with $1,200,000, which he invested in twenty-six short films to be shown on both sides of the Atlantic. Pat, playing an actress, was in episode 17, *Farewell Performance,* which was aired on 3 November 1956. Her co-stars were Ivan Craig and Conrad Phillips, the actor who played William Tell in the long running series of the same name during the late 1950s.

Pat, for whom financial security was always of paramount importance, juggled a number of rich suitors whenever she could. They included Jack Morrison, and Peter Lorne. Pat got to know Morrison, a millionaire property developer and entrepreneur, when she was filming *Farewell Performance* at Bray film studios, near Maidenhead. It was particularly handy for her, staying with her sister Marie-Louise who lived just around the corner from the studios. Morrison also lived in Bray, in a large house by the Thames where he moored his motor launch. He knew, and got on well with Pat's father, and it was through this friendship that Pat and Morrison met.

Scottish by birth, Morrison, who was single and quite a bit older than Pat, was an unlikely beau for a woman who was still considered to be one of the most attractive in London. He was opinionated, and physically unprepossessing. On the other hand, he made Pat laugh. He was one of the most amusing men that she had ever met and they complimented each other admirably. As for Jack Morrison, he was struck by her intelligence, her affectionate nature and above all, her total lack of pretension.

There was never any hint of seriousness about their relationship – they never cohabited for instance - but they did see a lot of one another, and were frequently seen abroad together on lavish holidays; Geneva and the South of France were popular haunts. It was more a romantic interlude than an affair.

Michael Thomas, Pat's son, speaks fondly about 'uncle Jack' (Michael had quite a few 'uncles' when he was young). "He was good to us and was a very generous person and it was apparent that he was doing everything he could to please Mama, even to the extent of making sure that I got a first class education. At the time I was going to North Bridge House School in Hampstead, but in 1959 he paid for me to go to Summer Fields Prep School in Oxford – that was a pretty expensive school and I thoroughly enjoyed it there. One of my best friends was Casper Fleming, the son of James Bond's creator, Ian Fleming. We were the same age and kept in touch after we left school. It came as quite a blow when I heard in 1973 that he had committed suicide. He was just 21." said Michael.

There was even more distressing news for Michael in 1973 when he got a telephone call from his mother to tell him that she had just heard that Jack Morrison had committed suicide following the recent economic slump. Reflecting on 'uncle' Jack, Michael said, "He lost a great deal of money when the bottom fell out of the property market. I remember Mama was pretty distraught because, although they hadn't seen much of one another for quite some time, she was still very fond of him – he was a good man and I got on well with him. There was one occasion however, when he was none too pleased with me. We all travelled down to Brighton in his Rolls Royce and I'm afraid I was sick in the back. I seem to remember, I was never allowed in that car again."

The affair with Peter Lorne was a little more serious; in fact it was a one hundred per cent love match. How they met, nobody is sure, but it would have been at the time Pat was seeing Jack Morrison. At this stage in her life, Pat did not feel the need to be discreet, as she had done when having affairs with the likes of Michael Wilding and Anthony Steel. Instead, she openly showed her affection for Lorne in public, without comment or denial, whether it was at a restaurant, theatre, or at film premieres, which she still attended. The fact that Lorne was married seemed not to matter to either of them.

Peter Lorne wasn't very tall, no more than a couple of inches taller than Pat, not unattractive but neither particularly handsome. Born in Chichester in 1916 into a middle-class family, he was almost a year younger than Pat, unusual in that she normally liked her gentlemen friends to be older. At the outbreak of war, he married Valerie Wilson who bore him two children. He then spent the war years in the Royal Navy. When he returned to Civvy Street he went into the lucrative advertising industry and became the European area manager of one of the World's top advertising agencies, McCann Erickson.

Everybody liked Peter. He was charming and easy-going, qualities that appealed to Pat, and his sense of humour was legendary. "He was another of my 'uncles', in fact my favourite and in many ways a surrogate dad, " recalled Michael, Pat's son. "He used to call me Mixa and was always cracking jokes. He had a wicked sense of humour."

As the affair intensified Lorne was intent on leaving his wife and two sons to be with Pat on a permanent basis. But after much anguished discussion they both reluctantly came to the same conclusion – that for the sake of Lorne's children who were no more than 10 to 13 years old, it would not be the right thing to do. Gradually they saw less and less of one another but during the time they were together, they laid the foundations of a lifelong friendship that lasted right up until his death in 1996 when he was eighty.

Career-wise, Pat may not have been particularly selective at this stage of her career, but she always maintained that no matter what the role was, she treated it with the utmost importance. This is how she approached her next film in 1957, *The House in the Woods,* an offbeat, little known hour long suspense-mystery thriller about a couple Carol (Patricia Roc) and her husband, Geoffrey Carter (Michael Gough) a writer, who go off into the country and rent a remote cottage. The aim was to get away from their noisy London apartment and find some peace and quiet so that he could work on his latest book. Their landlord at the cottage is Spencer Rowland, played by Ronald Howard, the son of Leslie Howard. Recently widowed, he begins to behave in a strange and menacing manner to the point where the Carters' suspect him of having murdered his wife, and about to do the same to Carol.

Written and directed by little heard of Maxwell Munden, the film was produced by Geoffrey Goodheart, and made at a small studio in St John's Wood, London. Like Cohen and Levy, Goodheart specialised in making low budget films during the 1950s, and it is to the credit of Pat, and the other two actors, Michael Gough and Ronald Howard, that they rose above the paltry budget and the short shooting schedule to give creditable performances. Pat in particular performed admirably with restraint and total professionalism, even though she later decried the film, claiming that she had never seen or particularly wanted to see it. Pity, it was quite a good little film, for what it was, even though it did have some strange and probably unintentionally amusing dialogue: "He's probably waiting out there until he thinks we've eaten the mushrooms" Carter says to his wife!

The *House in the Woods* was released in November 1957. Two months later, Pat was again seen on the small screen, this time in an episode of *The White Hunter* adventure series. It starred American actor Rhodes Reason playing John A. Hunter, a big game hunter. Most of the action was supposed to have taken place in Africa but it was in fact filmed at the Twickenham Studios in Middlesex, with African scenes taken from 'stock' footage. It would be almost two years before she got another acting job. She knew that now, well past 40, she faced the distinct possibility of disappearing altogether from the screen, large and small, unless something really impressive and important came along. In 1959 she thought that `something` had arrived when she was sent the script for *Bluebeard's Ten Honeymoons.* Then she read it and realised that it was, as she said, "Nothing much."

The star of the film was Pat old acquaintance George Sanders, a strange man, who in 1937 when he was 31, told David Niven that he would commit suicide when he was 65. He did just that thirty-four years later, on 23 April 1972, after losing a lot of money that he had invested into a sausage producing company. He checked into a hotel in Barcelona and was found dead two days later, having consumed five bottles of barbiturates. Having worked with him before in *Captain Blackjack*, Pat knew what to expect, and got it in the form of indifferent acting. "His heart just wasn't in it," said Pat, which wasn't really surprising. In his autobiography *Memoirs of a Professional Cad* published in 1960, he sardonically wrote:

'My loyal and devoted agent of twenty-five years' standing, William Shiffrin, negotiated a deal for me to play the lead in a picture called *Bluebeard's Ten Honeymoons* opposite Corinne Calvet. The picture was to be shot at the New Elstree Studios in London. I remember that some years ago Hollywood's great director Billy Wilder made a picture called *Bluebeard's Eighth Wife*, starring Gary Cooper and Claudette Colbert, and I assumed that this was going to be some sort of remake. When I heard that the director was going to be none other than Willie Wilder, I was convinced. When I heard that the cast was to include Monroe and Mansfield, I was enthusiastic. I must confess I found it rather hard to believe that Corinne Calvet was to be billed above Monroe and Mansfield, but since it has never been my practice to pay attention to the box-office fluctuations of Hollywood luminaries, I didn't allow the matter to exercise my mind. It was not until I arrived in London that I was to discover that Willie Wilder was Billy Wilder's brother, and that the cast, headed by Calvert, consisted not Marilyn and Jayne, but Elizabeth Monroe and Violet Mansfield imperceptibly supporting a number of professionally moribund actresses, all of whom in one way or another, I was to murder during the course of the picture. It seemed to me that in a way I was being called upon to perform a service to the community that newspaper critics for all their efforts, had still been unable to achieve.'

Those supporting actresses Sanders uncharitably referred to were Maxine Audley, Greta Gynt, Jean Kent and of course Patricia Roc. Pat knew all of these actresses well, but didn't get the chance to exchange any 'gossip' about Sanders with them. She was confined to just one segment of the film, which took less than three days to film, and involved scenes played with only Sanders. Consequently she didn't bump into any of the other 'girls' at the studios. Years later, Jean Kent, confessed that she didn't even know that her friend Pat was even in the film.

Although she didn't know it at the time, *Bluebeard's Ten Honeymoons* was Pat's swan song as far as the big screen was concerned. Interviewed by the *Sunday Express* about her contribution in the film, Pat said;

"Oh, it's not marvellous of course, but it is a start. I realise I can't hope for big parts. People have forgotten me. But I'm going to make a determined effort to get back." Asked if she thought that she jeopardised her career by marrying and going to France she unhesitatingly replied; "Oh yes. People got the impression that I had retired. Now my name no longer springs to mind when a film is being cast. Producers have such short memories. That is why I must take what work I can – to be seen. What I would really like is a television series. That would really get me re-established quicker than anything. Or one good part. That's all you need, one good part."

Pat did get more television work in the way of supporting roles, but not the series she had hoped for. She was cast in an episode of Associated Television's popular series *No Hiding Place*. She played the role of Mrs Ottlone, the wife of a wealthy South American millionaire. The episode called 'Who is Gustar Varna' was shown over the Christmas period in 1959. This was followed by an appearance in June 1960 in an episode of *Skyport*, a half-hour drama series set against the background of a large airport. It was made by Granada Television, with George Moon, an airport security man, the main stay of the series.

Pat's fans had to wait almost a year before she popped up on the television again, when she was seen in 'A Kiss for the Constable', one of the 432 episodes of that beloved British series, *Dixon of Dock Green*. One of the regulars of the series was Peter Byrne who, for twenty-one years, played Detective Sergeant Andy Crawford.

"I couldn't believe it when I saw Pat on the set. I often wondered what had happened to her, and there she was." said Peter Byrne in 2009. "As a teenager I used to idolise her, I thought she was the most beautiful woman on earth. I remember I was filming some wartime documentary at the Shepherds Bush studios the same time that Pat was there, I think she was making *The Wicked Lady*, and whenever I could, I would sneak into the studio where she was filming just to watch her. And do you know, she was just as beautiful when I saw her in 1960."

Then came a part that in theory should have got Pat's career on track for the come-back she so craved. Instead, it turned out to be the last professional acting job she ever did. In 1961 producers Bob Baker and Monty Berman cast

Pat in the first episode of Lew Grade's new TV series *The Saint*, which starred Roger Moore in the title role. Pat played the part of Madge Clarron, a rich woman married to a former actor and money-losing producer, nicely played by Derek Farr. He is trying to slowly poison his wife for her money. Madge's friend is The Saint who goes to visit her, now an invalid after a household accident. Titled 'The Talented Husband', it was shown on British TV on 4 October 1962.

Pat, who plays all her scenes confined to her bed, puts in a nuanced performance and was astonishingly good in the role, so why, it has to be asked, didn't it lead to further offers of work? In her infamous autograph book which she still kept, Derek Farr wrote: *Dear Pat, After all these years at last I've worked with you, I've loved it. Here's to the next time.* He never did work with Pat again, nobody did; the world of producers and casting directors is a strange and mysterious one.

Also in *The Talented Husband* was James Bond girl, Shirley Eaton. She played an insurance investigator called Adrienne who helps The Saint to apprehend John Clarron before he is able to do away with his wife. In her autobiography, *Golden Girl*, Miss Eaton wrote;

'In the first ever Saint episodes Patricia Roc was one of the guest stars. Patricia had been one of the truly glamorous stars of British movies of the forties and fifties, appearing in *Madonna of the Seven Moons, The Wicked Lady, The Brothers, Jassy, The Perfect Woman* and numerous others...*The Wicked Lady* caused quite a stir because of the supposed lowness of the necklines Patricia Roc and Margaret Lockwood wore. The Americans, in particular, got all steamed up about the amount of bosom the two British stars were showing. Judged by what contemporary actresses have to expose, Patricia Roc and Margaret Lockwood, two of the most glamorous stars of their day, were showing very little. But they didn't have to: glamour isn't about exposure, it's about beauty and taste and style. Patricia Roc had a lot of it and still had by the time she was in the Saint episode with me.'

Pat was still living in the Dorset House apartment when she made her appearance in *The Saint*. Another resident, living on the second floor was divorcee Walter Reif, a man of considerable wealth. He was Austrian, having been born in Vienna in 1909. Frequently they would bump into one another in the lift and exchange pleasantries. Then one day, Walter invited Pat to his apartment to look at his extensive and valuable art collection. *There is a joke somewhere there.* Art was always one of Pat's great passions in life, and her knowledge and appreciation of what was good and what was bad, impressed Walter so much, that whenever he went away on business he would ask her to look after his paintings for him.

Inevitably Pat and Walter became close and it wasn't too long before they were down at the Marylebone Register Office - on 5 September 1964 - to get married. Unlike the Peter Lorne affair however, for Pat, this was a friendship borne out of security. Whilst she wasn't exactly on 'the bread line', Pat wasn't a particularly wealthy lady. For sure, she had earned good money during the height of her career when she was a Gainsborough star, but like all high earners, in those days she paid a staggering 19s 6d in the pound income tax. She was still living in a style to which she had long been accustomed and was finding it difficult to maintain now that her acting career had come to a standstill. She was not of course alone in marrying for security. Across the 'pond', Joan Crawford, Bette Davis, Greer Garson and Jennifer Jones all counted business tycoons amongst their husbands. As for Walter, he got what he wanted, a glamorous 'trophy wife' on his arm when he entertained his well-heeled clients, whilst Pat got the financial security she felt she needed.

Michael Thomas was 11 and still a pupil at Summer Fields when his mother married Walter. "I don't think Walter liked children very much," said Michael. "We had a middling relationship to say the least, but I made the effort for Mama's sake. I had more of a rapport with 'uncle' Peter than I ever did with Walter. Peter used to phone me up, long after he and Mama stopped being an item, and take me out to lunch. After he left McCann Erickson he became Chairman of Studio Film Laboratories in Soho, a major post-production house, and it was through that, that he got me a stint at Rank Laboratories in Denham in the early 1970s after I had left school. I stuck it out for eighteen months and decided it wasn't really for me, but it was good of him to take the trouble to get me started and wasn't a bit resentful that I didn't stick it out. That was the sort of person he was. He was a most likeable man. Walter, on the other hand, did not take kindly to me leaving, after a year, a job he arranged for me in Johannesburg in 1975 when I was 23. He thought that I was very ungrateful to say the least."

After an extended honeymoon at Walter's holiday apartment at Ascona in Switzerland, the couple bought an apartment at The Athenaeum, beside Hampstead Heath in the Vale of Health. Pat enjoyed living there. She could walk her dogs on the Heath and it wasn't too far from central London where she still liked to shop for clothes – but she still missed the excitement she got from acting. "Walter doesn't want me to work really," she told journalist and next-door neighbour Rosemarie Wittman. "We do so much entertaining. It's a different life." It may have been a different life but she would still have liked to have stood in front of a camera again, and had it not been for Walter's autocratic attitude, gradually cutting her off from the life she had once knew, she most probably would have found work. "Ideally," she told Wittman, "I would love to work in a comedy on the stage."

Michael had now left Summer Fields and went straight on to Stowe in Buckinghamshire, a leading public school where three decades earlier David Niven had been educated. "I was there from 1965 to 1969. I think Walter was pleased to have me out of the way, but it didn't matter to me. I was never naturally drawn to him, and I never saw him as a father figure. As for Stowe, I loved it there," said Michael.

Occasionally Pat received television offers that she would discuss with Walter only to have him reject them. It was as if he was trying, and it could be argued with some success, to exercise total control of her life. If he was, Pat was not willing to forego the opportunity of being a surprise guest when Eamonn Andrews ambushed Margaret Lockwood for his BBC *This is Your Life* series in November 1963. Neither could he stop her appearing on Thames Television nine years later to surprise Phyllis Calvert, who was also the subject of the *This is Your Life* series. Pat, Margaret and Phyllis were always regarded as the Gainsborough girls, the main stay of that company's much revered costume melodramas, although each in their own way were quite different. It was always said that at Gainsborough:

'If you open Miss Calvert's dressing-room door you'll see pots and pans, shopping lists, recipe books. Dogs' leads and children's toys.'
'If you open Miss Lockwood's dressing-room door you'll see a picture of Toots (her daughter), and a script.'
'If you open Miss Roc's dressing-room door you'll see a divan furnished with satin cushions, mascot dolls, cut-glass perfume bottles and flowers.'

Regardless of what Walter said or thought, there was no way that Pat was going to 'snub' either, on their special evening. It is strange and somewhat remiss that the television companies did not accord the same tribute to Pat. Had they have done so, there would have been an endless supply of her contemporaries willing to speak about the warm, generous person Pat always was to everybody she ever worked with.

She could never have been accused of being narcissistic, but throughout her life she loved to be with people, and loved to be liked. In her heyday she was constantly in demand, and always invited and welcomed everywhere. But now, she was living a totally different life and retreated more and more into anonymity from the cinematic world. Having resigned herself to the fact that her acting days were over, she settled down to married life with Walter, wondering, nostalgically, what might have been. It didn't help when she watched Margaret Lockwood's success in the TV series *Justice*, which aired for the first time in October 1971. She wasn't jealous, that was a word that was not in Pat's vocabulary. She just wished that she could have done something similar.

***

On October 20, 1973, *The Times* newspaper carried the announcement in its 'Deaths' column;

> André Magnus Riese
> On 18th 1973. Peacefully after a long illness André Riese of 32 Bryanston Square, W1. Beloved husband of Barney and father of Bunny, Bobby and Marie-Louise. Cremation Golders Green, Thursday 21 June at 3pm.

Her father had been ill for some time and had been nursed by Clarence (for some odd reason, known to all as 'Barney') his second wife. She was a widow whom André had married in 1961. She was no friend of the family however, and was referred to as 'that woman' by Pat's sister Bobby, who claimed that she was interested in nothing more than her father's money. After the funeral she was never seen again by any of 'the Riese girls'.

Pat was devastated when her father died. He had given her so much support over the years, and even though he hadn't wanted her to become an actress way back in 1937, he was always tremendously proud of her achievements. His death affected her badly and it was about this time that she began to sink into a state of depression, which unquestionably contributed to an act that was to cause Pat deep regret and embarrassment, and infuriate Walter.

Pat and André on their wedding day. Behind André with the British flag is Terence Young and behind Pat, waving the French flag is Jean Dréville. (Courtesy of Michael Thomas)

Script conference between Herbert Marshall, Pat, Agnes Moorhead and George Sanders during the making of 'Black Jack' (Author's Private Collection)

*"He was very good in bed," said Patricia Roc about her co-star, Anthony Steel
when making 'Something Money Can't Buy'.
(ITV Studios Global International)*

Looking a bit worried! Pat in 'Son Copain' (Author's Private Collection)

Time for a cup of tea with Jacque Tourneur during the making of 'Circle of Danger' (Kobal Collection)

Patricia Roc with Massimo Serato in 'The Widow' (Author's Private Collection

Paul Carpenter kisses Pat in The Hypnotist' (Authors Private Collection)

Easter 1954 in Rome – Pat with her young son Michael.
This was the last time André saw him.
(Courtesy of Michael Thomas)

Pat with Peter Lorne and 'a friend' (Courtesy of Michael Thomas)

Pat with Michael Gough in 'House in the Woods' (Author's Private Collection)

George Sanders gets to grips with Patricia Roc in 'Bluebeard's Ten Honeymoons'
(Courtesy of Michael Thornton)

The 'Riese' girls with their father, from left: Bobby, Pat, Marie-Louise and André Riese
(Courtesy of Michael Thomas)

CHAPTER FIFTEEN

Unwelcome Publicity

THE eleventh of February 1975, the day that was a triumph for Margaret Thatcher when she was elected leader of the Conservative Party - the first woman to become head of a major British political party - was anything but a triumph for Patricia Roc, when she was accused of shoplifting. The undignified event began when she went on her own to the West End in the morning to do some routine shopping, calling in at the Oxford Street branch of one of Britain's favourite stores, Marks and Spencer. There, she went to the toiletry department, selected a bottle of bubble bath and some small boxes of tissues, and put them into her bag without paying. When she was leaving the store, a female store detective who had recognised the actress stopped her. Told that she had goods worth £1.45 [about £9] on her that she hadn't paid for, Pat simply replied; "Have I? I'm sorry". Two policemen were called and took Pat to the West End Central Police Station where she was charged with theft.

The following day, wearing a green raincoat and matching headscarf, she appeared at Marylebone Street Magistrates Court and, having been ill advised to plead guilty to avoid unnecessary publicity, she was fined £25 [about £170]. Prosecuting, Mr. James Bullen told the court that Pat, who received £25 a week allowance for housekeeping, had over £12 [£80 in her purse when she was arrested, and had £50 [£345] savings in an account. Throughout the Court hearing Pat remained silent. When it was over she took a taxi to back to her home in Hampstead to face her irate husband who was not with her in Court. Pat was more angry than humiliated, for being advised – by her husband's solicitor - to plead guilty. "I'm not a thief, it was a simple mistake on my behalf," she said years later.,

Appearing under her married name Felicia Reif, it was hoped, especially by Walter, that she would not be recognised as the actress Patricia Roc, but the press boys were not to be fooled. As soon as they got wind of it, they had a field day and the case was splashed all over the newspapers the following day. 'Patricia Roc, housewife and fallen angel, is fined for shoplifting', was the *Daily Express* headline and was typical of those in other national dailies.

It may have been some consolation to have known that she was not the first or last celebrated name to have suffered the humiliation of a being accused of shoplifting. Among them was Wyn Jones, a former police officer once tipped as a possible chief of the Metropolitan Police. She was convicted in 1995 of stealing food and wine worth £24 [£35] from Marks and Spencer. Then there was Hollywood star Hedy Lamarr, who was accused of helping herself to a number of items including a knitted suit, knickers and makeup from a May Department Store (now Macy's) in 1966. Even Jeffrey Archer was accused of leaving a store in Toronto in 1975 with three suits he hadn't paid for. When he explained that he hadn't realised that he had actually left the store, the police dropped the charges. But sadly for Lady Isobel Barnet, a doctor, magistrate and panellist on the popular 1950s and 1960s television show, *What's My Line*, the shame of prosecution was too much. She killed herself in October 1980, four days after she had been convicted of shoplifting goods worth 87p [£3].

Amidst all the furore over the Isobel Barnet case, the late *Daily Mail* columnist, Lynda Lee-Potter said she had interviewed dozens of alleged women shoplifters who set up a strong pattern: most were widowed or emotionally neglected by their husbands, and they felt no sense of dishonesty; the thefts were an escape from monotony and depression, and occasionally were sexually arousing. According to Lee-Potter, one woman told her, "I got an orgasm every time I slipped something into my handbag."

In the case of Pat's indiscretion in the Marks and Spencer store, it was more likely to have been the result of her depression, brought on by her father's death and having been cut off, rather brutally, from her former friends in the film and theatre world. This was particularly true in the 1970s when she was only seen once at a show business occasion – the Thanksgiving Service for the life of her dear friend, Dennis Price, at St. Paul's, Covent Garden (the Actor's Church), on 27 November 1973, when she sat with her former lover, Michael Wilding.

There is no doubt that Pat was now desperately missing the glamour and excitement of her former days when she was Rank's *goddess,* and was constantly telling anybody willing to listen how much she regretted giving up her film career. "I wouldn't have missed one minute of my life in show business. My only regret is that it didn't continue." She told a *Sunday Express* reporter.

Needless to say, Walter was furious with all the publicity his wife's conviction garnered. He took it personally, even, it has been suggested, suspecting that Pat had gone out shoplifting to belittle him, which she most certainly didn't. His immediate response was to leave the country. For some time he had been toying with the idea of moving abroad to avoid paying the high rate of income tax levied on high earners by the then Labour Government. Now his mind was made up. He made arrangements to move to Minusio near the Swiss resort of Locarno. Walter already had a small holiday apartment there, which he sold, and bought a much larger apartment with its own secluded garden overlooking Lake Maggiore. It was close to where Pat was on location when she made *One Night With You* in 1947. She was to live there for the rest of her life.

At first Pat was reluctant to go, after all, her friends and family were in England, but Walter insisted and by mid-1975, Mr. and Mrs. Rief had moved to Switzerland, where presumably he could hold his head up high once again. He gave up his post as Managing Director of Combined Shipping and Trading in London, and worked from his new home in Minusio, managing several well-healed clients' investment portfolios, and making weekly trips to Zurich. As for Pat, she now lived the way Walter wanted her to live, and became a popular local resident, rather than a star. She seldom discussed her former career, although there were occasions when a fan would recognise her in the street and want to stand and talk to her...then she was in her element, not out of bravado, but merely to recall the happy days she had spent making films.

She now made new friends, including American film actress Paulette Goddard. At the height of her career Goddard was considered for the role of Scarlett O'Hara in the 1939 film *Gone With the Wind,* but she eventually lost the part to Vivien Leigh. Like Pat, her film career faded in the late 1940s, making a just a handful of 'best forgotten' films in the 1950s. She married Charlie Chaplin in 1936, well, they lived together as husband and wife, although their marital status was always a source of controversy. From 1944 to 1949 she was married to Burgess Meredith and it was during this marriage, when Burgess was making *Man on the Eiffel Tower* in Paris that Pat first met and became friends with Paulette. In 1958 she married the German author, Erich Paul Remarque, and moved to Locarno.

"I knew Paulette well, she lived close by in a beautiful house by the lake. We lunched and dined together fairly frequently," remembered Pat. "She always looked great but tried her best to still be the film star, in her manner and dress. It was a pity she found it so difficult to grow old gracefully," she added.

One particular dinner party which Pat and Paulette attended stood out in Pat's memory. Shortly after they had arrived for drinks, Paulette suddenly announced: "I'm going into the kitchen because it's time we ate." Some minutes later she reappeared and said: "Well, we can eat now." After finishing the main course, the party sat back to enjoy a brief interlude prior to the dessert course, when Paulette abruptly stood up and announced: "Well, I can't wait any longer. I have to go home. You know I have to go to bed early." The hostess protested that the dessert had been made especially for her, but Paulette was adamant. "She didn't say goodbye to anybody," Pat recalled, "Just stood up and walked out. I found it so ill-mannered." Pat was quite the opposite. Her upbringing had taught her to display good manners no matter what the situation, and she did.

***

In 1980 Pat was invited, with scores of other stars, to appear in London Weekend Television's *Night of 100 Stars Gala*. It was staged to mark the fiftieth anniversary of the founding of the British Actors Equity with monies raised going to various theatrical charities. Compered by Terry Wogan, the show was recorded on 14 December at the National Theatre and shown on national television over the Christmas holiday.

"And now ladies and gentlemen," announced Wogan, "the glamour girl of my youth and the movie goddess of a million dreams, the fabulous Patricia Roc." Pat walked slowly onto the stage, curtseyed to the audience and to Princess Margaret in the Royal Box, and then saw that the people were rising to their feet. She stretched out her arms, as if to embrace the audience, blew several kisses around the auditorium, and mouthed the words, "Thank you", though she would never have been heard, such was the roar. It was the sort of reception normally reserved for pop stars and it was several minutes before Wogan could make himself heard, and the show could move on. Pat was naturally quite overcome; it had been twenty years since she had made her last film, but it showed what a tremendous affection the public still had for her. Backstage, she broke down in tears. Anna Neagle put her arms around her and said, "Once a star, Darling, always a star – always recognised and remembered with love." The only other person to receive such a welcome that evening was Jessie Matthews, who was suffering from terminal cancer. She sang 'When You've Got A Little Springtime In Your Heart'. It was her last public appearance. She died eight months later.

Back stage after the 'Night of 100 Stars Gala' Patricia Roc was overcome by the warm reception she received and burst into tears. She was comforted by Dame Anna Neagle seen here, holding Pat's hand (Courtesy of Michael Thornton)

It was at that Gala that Pat met up with Anthony Steel. There had been little communication between the two of them ever since they completed *Something Money Can't Buy*, other than for Pat to inform Steel that he had a son called Michael. She thought it was now time, and Steel agreed, that Michael, now 28, should be told the truth about his real father. "I was living in Cape Town at the time and I remember Mama and I went out to dinner one evening", said

Michael. "Mama casually said, `Of course, you realise that you are a love child don't you'? I was quite taken aback to discover (as his mother had done before him) that I wasn't who I thought I was. I obviously knew who Anthony Steel was from the movies he'd made and I remember thinking at the time that I'd wished I had known when I was at school that he was my dad. Being the son of a superstar would have boosted my *street cred* no end."

One of Michael's biggest regrets was that he didn't get to meet or ever speak to his father. He was living and working in Cape Town until 1986, during which time Steel was under-employed making one-off appearances in television series like *Robin Hood of Sherwood*, and *Bergerac*. When this work dried up, almost penniless by the end of the 1980s, Steel moved from his one room in a modest Earl's Court hotel to council sheltered accommodation in Northolt, West London. For several years he just vanished from the radar screen. When he was eventually found in the late 1990s by a Sunday tabloid, his agent, David Daly, arranged for him to go into Denville Hall, the care home for elderly actors. There, he was cleaned and patched up, and Daly even found him work in 1999 for the television series, *The Broker's Man*. By the time that Michael Thomas learnt that his father was in Denville Hall, Steel was suffering from terminal cancer. Michael went there in the hope that his father would see him, but Steel was too ill to receive visitors. He died in March 2001. His son had the sad experience of attending the funeral of the father he had never known.

Patricia Roc with her son, Michael in the early 1980s (Courtesy of Michael Thornton)

Pat and Walter Reif, her third husband, on their wedding day.
(Courtesy of Michael Thomas)

Pat, shortly after her eightieth birthday, still looking incredibly slim and youthful.
(Courtesy of Michael Thornton)

CHAPTER SIXTEEN

The Final Years

AS THE 1980s progressed, Pat settled into her changed way of life. "I do miss the theatre and avidly read all I can about it, but La Scala in Milan isn't far. We also have a film festival in Locarno for two weeks in August, although I must say, so many of the actors and actresses are new to me now. I also read the *International Herald Tribune* and *Time Magazine* to keep me up to date with all the news art-wise, theatre-wise, as well as worldwide, so I don't feel at all cut off from my former way of living," Pat told Michael Thornton.

But in spite of her assurances, Pat did very often feel cut off and isolated in Minusio, particularly after Walter's death in 1986. He had been diagnosed with cancer. It is true that for both of them, it was a marriage of convenience, never sharing the same bedroom, let alone the same bed, but over the years they were married, Pat had grown fond of Walter and had relied on him so much. That same year, in March, her youngest sister Marie-Louise died at the age of 61. Her smoking habit finally having caught up with her, she developed lung cancer. This crippling illness had taken two of the most important people in Pat's life and now, she felt on her own.

When Walter died, he left an estate worth £6.5 million [£15,000,000} much of which was given away in his will, leaving Pat to live off the interest in an escrow account that ultimately went to his niece and nephew on her death. For a time she contemplated moving back to England, but the thought of having her two dogs and cats put into quarantine for six months put paid to that idea. Perhaps for all her three husbands, her pets – each one in turn being her favourite - were the passion of her life.

Pat loved London, "Being a Londoner I shall always love her no matter what," she said, "but being older, when I was last there, I found there was too much traffic, too much noise, and too many people. Quite a big difference to where I live now. It is known as Camellia Country because of the huge variety of camellias that grow here, some like trees. It really is a beautiful place right next to the lake and surrounded by mountains. I'm really very content and treat each day as a bonus."

Michael Thomas would visit his mother whenever possible, but he was always travelling, invariably on the other side of the world. He married South African super model, Louise Lapman in August 1983, a marriage that Pat tried in vain to talk him out of, not because she disliked Louise, quite the contrary, but she didn't want Michael making the same mistakes she had made. As it turned out, Pat was proved right; the marriage didn't last. He is now with Alison Forbes, whom he met in Singapore in 1995 when he was on a round the world trip. "I literally gate crashed her leaving party when she was about to return to the UK," said Michael. Since then they have travelled all over the world together and set up a beach holiday complex at Tangalle, Sri Lanka. They now have a daughter, whom Alison named Steele Sapphire, in memory of Michael's father, Anthony Steel. "Sadly," said Michael, "my mother never got to meet her granddaughter. She would have been so proud of her."

Pat's final appearance ever, in front of an audience, came in 1996 when she appeared on Chili Bouchier's *This is Your Life* programme. Beautifully dressed and wonderfully poised at the recording, it was clear that all her years of stardom had kept her professional instincts completely intact. Three years later, the National Film Theatre honoured Pat with a short season of three of her films, *Perfect Woman, When the Bough Breaks* and *One Night with You*. Introducing her, the programme notes read; 'The '40s was a golden age for British female stars, with Patricia Roc one of the most popular'. When told about this, she said, "I hope people still enjoy my pictures. When I watch myself as I was all those years ago it all comes flooding back to me. You forget the plots and the situations, but as each scene comes up I remember why they couldn't fit this and that in and even who the make up girl was. Every now and again I still look through my autograph book. It's so sad, most of my friends in it are no longer with us – they've all gone."

The death of Christine Norden in 1988 affected her greatly. So did the deaths of Kenneth More in 1982 and Laurence Olivier in 1989. Both had been close friends. But perhaps the saddest of all was the passing of Gordon Jackson in 1990. "He was such a beautiful actor and a really lovely man," she said. "He sent me a copy of a piece that a film historian had written about *Millions Like*

Us, saying that our love scenes together, showing two inarticulate working-class characters attempting to express their feelings for each other, were not to be equalled until the 'kitchen sink' films came along in the 1960s. We were both amazed by that and also quite proud."

Margaret Lockwood's death, six months after Jackson's, seemed to Pat to bring down the curtain on a whole era of British cinema. Their former publicist, Theo Cowan, arranged the Thanksgiving Service at St. Paul's, Covent Garden for Margaret, and repeatedly urged Pat to attend. She pleaded a prior engagement in Locarno, but it seemed that she simply could not face such an occasion, even though Phyllis Calvert and Jean Kent were both to give readings. She sent personal messages to Julia Lockwood, Margaret's daughter, and to Phyllis and Jean, but she did not attend the service. "It was such a bright, vivid and happy era at Gainsborough," she said. "I would like to remember it as it was and not mourn its passing".

The 'prior engagement' that kept Pat from attending Lockwood's memorial service was a lunch for fifty people, which she had arranged to celebrate the twentieth anniversary of the local International Club. Its members were expatriates from eighteen different countries, who had settled in the area. For five years Pat was the Clubs president.

The worst blow of all was the death of Phyllis Calvert in October 2002. "Now they have almost all gone," she said. "Dennis Price, James Mason, Maggie (Margaret Lockwood), Stewart Granger, and now Phyl. Only Jean Kent and I are left. Suddenly it makes one aware of one's age and mortality".

Pat wanted to live long enough to receive the congratulatory card from Her Majesty the Queen for reaching 100. She missed that ambition by twelve years. Following the death of Phyllis Calvert, Pat seemed to give in to her 87 years as her health began to decline. She now rarely left the apartment. A nursing agency came in daily to check on her, whilst her young housekeeper, Karen, would do her shopping and cook her meals. Pat now spent her days reading, listening to music, and occasionally she would stroll around her garden. But her daily walk into nearby Locarno to the town was a thing of the past.

In November 2003 Pat developed peritonitis and almost died. The hospital in Locarno was able to get her through that, but she was now a very frail lady. After five weeks in hospital Pat went into a coma and died peacefully in her sleep in the early hours of the morning on the day before New Year's Eve, with Michael at her bedside. Pat was cremated in Minusio. Eighty of her local friends attended the funeral, and even then, many of them were still unaware of her importance and eminence as a box-office star during the post war years.

Patricia Roc was radiantly beautiful, a talented actress, a woman of tremendous sexual charisma. She was the epitome of effortless style, class, refinement and grace. She was intelligent, intuitive, with breeding. She lived, she said, three lives - first her youth, which to her seemed gloriously carefree; then the film star days, with all the adulation that went with that, the endless fan mail, the personal appearances, the screaming crowds, being mobbed as she got out of the car and having to be protected by police in order to get into the cinema; and finally her life in Switzerland, which to her, seemed so peaceful by contrast. "Each life," she said, "overlapping and yet each one separate. I think I have been a very lucky woman."

Pat's ashes were brought over from Switzerland by her son and interred in the grave of her parents and sister, Marie-Louise (Courtesy of Michael Thomas)

Appendix

A small selection of autographs collected by Patricia Roc during her days as an actress

Anthony Steel
Duncan Macrea
Roger Moore
Ray Milland
Phyllis Calvert
Bill Owen
Honor Blackman
George Formby
Derek Farr
Charles Laughton
Reneé Houston
Flora Robson
Donald Stewart
Lloyd Bridges
Margaret Lockwood
George Sanders
Stanley Holloway
Leslie Arliss
Michael Wilding
Kay Wilding
James Mason
Cyril Hartman
Susan Hayward
Stewart Granger
Sidney Gilliat
Jean Drevillé
Dana Andrews

Pat darling
This has been one picture I wish perhaps could have <u>well</u>
gone over schedule – you have helped to make it such a warm, pleasing eight weeks for
all of us in it.
Unfortunately your company is 'Something Money Can't Buy in any currency.
Perhaps we shall make another together, I can't wish for more.
With every considerably affection & love,
'Harry Wilding'
Perhaps more simply – All my love Pat, Tony Steel 30/3/52

Whilst making *Something Money Can't Buy* together, Pat and Steel embarked on an affair resulting in the birth of Pat's only child. Pat rarely saw Steel after filming was complete.

Go to your bed alone!
John Duncan Macrae
'The Brothers' Aug '46

A knowing comment from Duncan Macrea referring to Pat's affair with the director of *The Brothers*, David MacDonald

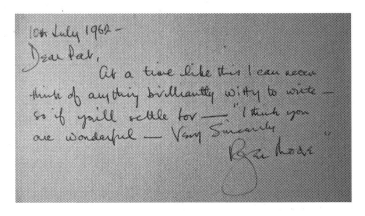

10th July 1962
Dear Pat,
At a time like this I can never think of anything brilliantly witty to write – so if you'll settle for – 'I think you are wonderful – Very sincerely Roger Moore'

Pat appeared in the very first *The Saint* television programme in which Roger Moore played the title role.

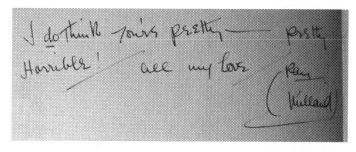

I <u>do</u> think you're pretty – pretty Horrible!
All my love
Ray (Milland)

Pat and Ray Milland stared in *Circle of Danger* together.

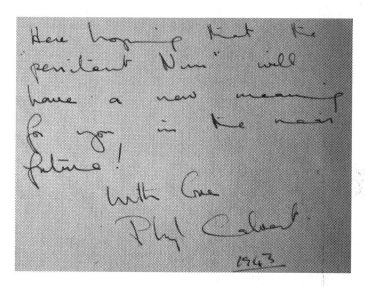

Here's hoping that the 'penitent Nun' will have a new meaning for you in the future!
With love Phyl Calvert <u>1943</u>

Phyllis Calvert signed Pat's book when they were making 2000 Women together. It is not known who Calvert's sarcastic comment was referring to!

Dear Pat
'WHEN THE BOUGH BREAKS' was a twofold 'break' for me. I played with you and
it was my biggest part in a film to date.
I ask one more 'break' that is to be able to play in lots more films with you.
With happy memories
Sincerely
Bill Rowbotham, 'Snow 47'

Bill Rowbotham changed his name to Bill Owen shortly after the film was
made and although he never made another picture with Pat, he enjoyed a
successful career which culminated with his portrayal of Compo in the long
running TV series *Last of the Summer Wine*. 'Snow 47' refers to the appalling
weather during filming *When the Bough Breaks.*

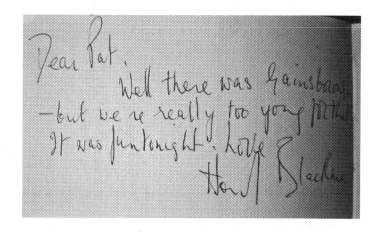

Dear Pat
Well there was Gainsborough – but we're really too young for that! It was fun tonight.
Love, Honor Blackman

When contacted, Honor Blackman claimed that she had never met Pat!

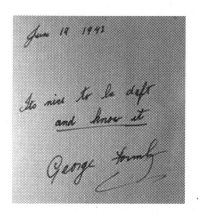

June 19 1942
It's nice to be daft <u>and know it</u>
George Formby

George Formby co-produced *Let the People Sing* in which Pat played the part of Miss Check

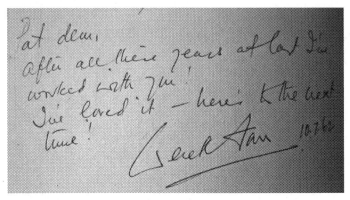

Pat dear,
After all these years at last I've worked with you!
I've loved it – here's to the next time!
Derek Farr   10.7.62

Derek Farr played Pat's husband in the very first episode of *The Saint*, which starred Roger Moore. Derek Farr who died in 1986, was married to Muriel Pavlow.

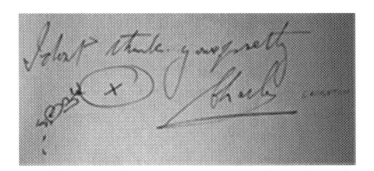

I don't think you're pretty Charles X

Charles Laughton, one of the many 'stars' Pat met in Hollywood, no doubt being witty. (Pat added LAUGHTON in pencil)

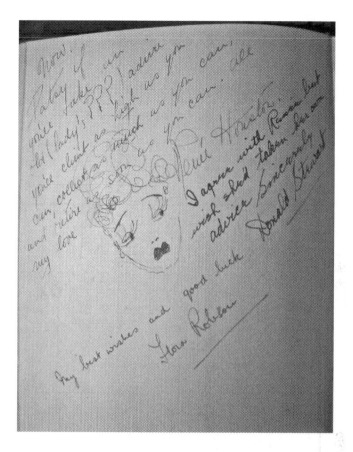

Now Patsy if you'll take an old (lady's???) advice you'll climb as <u>high</u> as you can,
collect as much as you can, and retire as soon as you can.
All my love
Reneé Houston

***

I agree with Reneé but wished she'd taken her own advice.
Sincerely
Donald Stewart

***

My best wishes and good luck
Flora Robson

These three autographs were collected during the making of *2000 Women*
which was filmed in 1943.

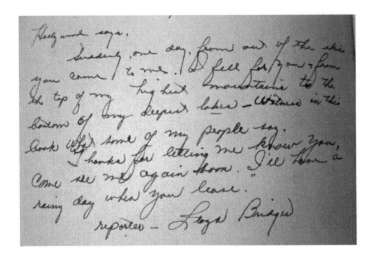

Hollywood saga.
'Suddenly one day from out of the skies you came to me. I fell for you from the top of
my highest mountain to the bottom of my deepest lakes – Witnessed in this book what
some of my people say. I thank you for letting me know you, come and see me again
soon. I'll have a rainy day when you leave.'
Reporter - Lloyd Bridges

Pat is on record as saying that Lloyd Bridges and his wife Dorothy were two of
the friendliest people when she was filming in Hollywood. It was rumoured
however that she and Bridges were more than just good friends!

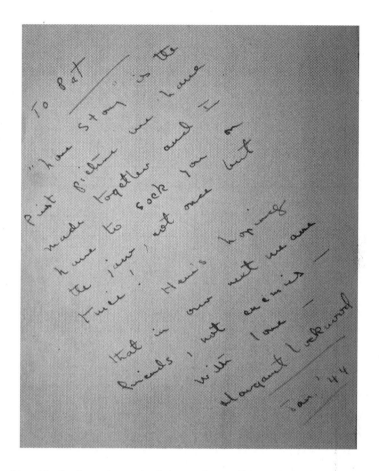

Love Story' is the first picture we have made together and I have to sock you on the jaw, not once but twice!
Here's hoping that in our next we are friends, not enemies –
With love
Margaret Lockwood
Jan '44

In their next picture together – *The Wicked Lady* – Pat wallops Margaret Lockwood, good and proper. But in spite of all this 'fighting' they were always the very best of friends in private life.

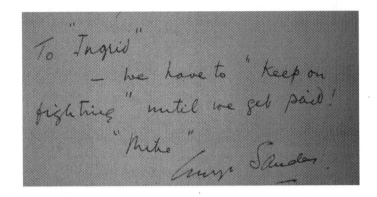

To 'Ingrid' We have to 'keep on fighting' until we get paid!
'Mike'
George Sanders

'Ingrid' was the character Pat played in *Black Jack*. George Sanders (his character name was 'Mike') is referring to the fact that none of the principal actors received any payment for their work.

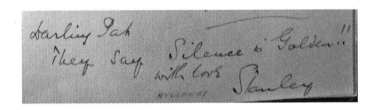

Darling Pat
They say Silence is Golden!!
With love
Stanley

Stanley Holloway (a man of few words) was in *The Perfect Woman* with Pat, the last film she made for the Rank Organisation as a contract player.

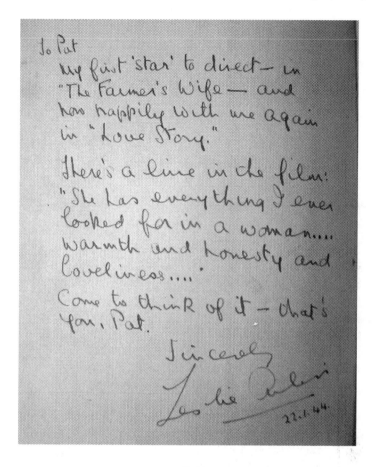

To Pat
My first 'star' to direct in 'The Farmers Wife' – and now happily with me again in
'Love Story'.
There's a line in the film: 'She has everything I ever looked for in a woman…warmth
and honesty and loveliness…'
Come to think of it – that's you Pat.
Sincerely
Leslie Arliss   22.1.44

Leslie Arliss directed Pat in *The Wicked Lady* too. He was not everybody's favourite director, but Pat adored him.

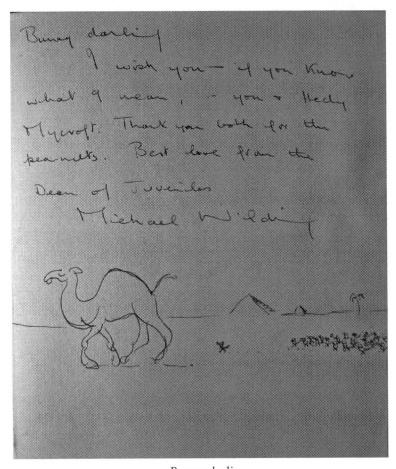

Bunny darling

I wish you – if you know what I mean, - you and Hechy Mycroft. Thank you both for
the peanuts. Best love from the Dean of Juveniles
Michael Wilding

'Bunny' was the name Pat's family and friends always called her. 'Hechy
Mycroft' was a reference to Walter Mycroft who produced *The Farmer's Wife* –
the film Pat and Wilding first met and fell in love.

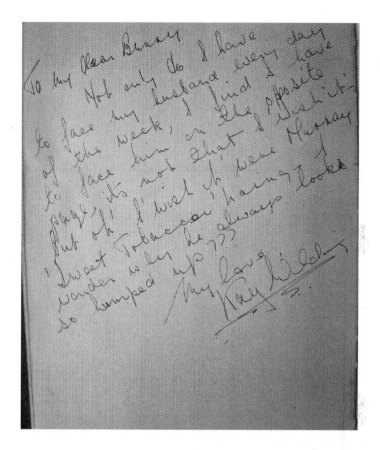

To my dear Bunny
Not only do I have to face my husband every day of the week, I find I have to face him
on the opposite page, its not that wish it – but Oh! I wish it were Murray 'Sweet
Tobacco' Laing – I wonder why he always looks so humped up???
My love
Kay Wilding

A slightly barbed message to Pat letting her know that she was fully aware of her husband and Pat's ongoing affair. Murray Laing of course was Pat's husband at that time.

Remember, my lad,
When you're feeling sad,
When you're losing your grip
When you've got the pip —
If you're just an old ham
And you don't give a damn,
And the ruddy scene's played
How you're paid —
So long as you're paid —
When your talent's ignored,
And you're thoroughly bored,
When you're dead on your feet
And your misry's complete —
This applies to you too
On the camera crew,
To the boy on the boom,
In the makeup room,
The carpenter's shop,
To the variable prop-
erty man & his mate,
To the man on the gate —
And when he's browned off is
The man in the office
Less likely to moan
That he's all on his own

7.7.0.

Continued next page

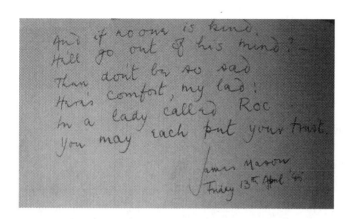

Remember, my lad,
When you're feeling sad,
When you're losing your grip
When you've got the pip –
If you're just an old ham
And you don't give a damn
How the ruddy scene's played
So long as you're paid –
When you're talents ignored
And you're thoroughly bored
When you're dead on your feet
And you're misery's complete –
This applies to you too
On the camera crew
To the boy on the boom,
In the makeup room,
The carpenter's shop,
To the venerable prop-
erty man and his mate,
To the man on the gate –
And when he's browned off is

The man in the office
Less likely to moan
That he's all on his own
And if no one is kind
He'll go out of his mind?-
Then don't be so sad
Here's comfort, my lad:
In a lady called Roc
You may each put your trust

James Mason
Friday 13 April 1945

You move, in grace and beauty, back through the centuries
to the age of Charles ll, and, for the time being, seem to belong there.
Fortunately for us you always have to come back to us again.
Cyril Hughes Hartman May 1945 'The Wicked Lady'

Cyril Hartman was the period advisor for the film *The Wicked Lady.*

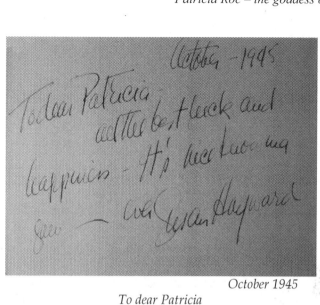

October 1945
To dear Patricia
All the best of luck and happiness – It's nice knowing you – ever
Susan Hayward

Pat and Susan Hayward were the two leading ladies in the film *Canyon Passage* which Pat made in Hollywood.

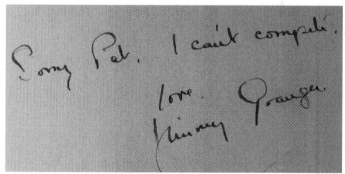

Sorry Pat, I can't compete., love
Jimmy Granger

Stewart (to his friends, Jimmy) Granger was another man of few word!

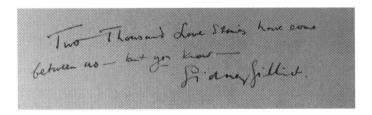

Two Thousand Love Stories have come between us – but you know –
Sidney Gilliat
Sidney Gilliat wrote and directed 2000 Women, Pat's first Gainsborough film as a contract artist. Did Gilliat have a secret 'crush' on Pat!!!

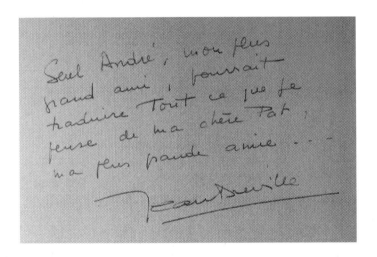

Only André, my greatest friend could translate
everything I think of my dear Pat my greatest friend…
Jean Dreville

Jean Drevillé was a French film director and a great friend of André (Thomas) who Pat married in 1949

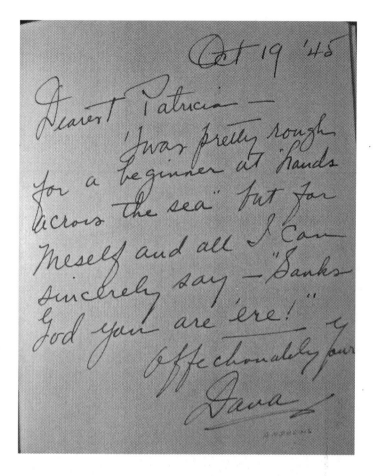

Oct 19 '45
Dearest Patricia –
I was pretty rough for a beginner at 'Hands across the sea' but for meself and all I can
sincerely say – Thanks God you are 'ere!'
Affectionately Yours
Dana

Dana Andrews played opposite Pat in the Hollywood film *Canyon Passage*.
(Underneath 'Dana' (Pat has written ANDREWS in pencil)

Filmography

The Rebel Son, (1938) London Films Omnia; Produced by E. C. Molinier **and Charles** David; Directed **by** Adrian Brunel, and Alexis Granowsky; Screenplay by Adrian Brunel based on a story by Nicolai Gogol. <u>Cast</u>: Harry Baur , Patricia Roc, Roger Livesey, Anthony Bushell, Joan Gardner, Frederick Culley.

The Gaunt Stranger, (1938) Northwood/Capad (Ealing); Produced by Michael Balcon; Directed by Walter Forde; Screenplay by Sidney Gilliat, based on the novel The Ringer by Edgar Wallace. <u>Cast</u>: Sonnie Hale, Wilfrid Lawson, Louise Henry, Alexander Knox, Patricia Roc, Patrick Barr , John Longden , Peter Croft, George Merritt, Arthur Hambling ,

A Window in London, (1939) G and S / GFD; Produced by Josef Somlo; Directed by Herbert Mason; Screenplay by Ian Darymple, and Brigid Cooper. <u>Cast</u>: Michael Redgrave, Patricia Roc, Sally Gray, Paul Lucas, Hartley Power.

The Mind of Mr Reeder, (1939) Jack Raymond Productions; Produced and Directed by Jack Raymond; Screenplay by Bryan Edgar Wallace, Marjorie Gaffney and Michael Hogan, based on a novel by Edgar Wallace. <u>Cast</u>: Will Fyffe, Patricia Roc, Kay Walsh, George Curzon, Chili Bouchier, John Warwick.

The Missing People, (1939) Grand National Pictures; Produced and Directed by Jack Raymond; Screenplay Lydia Hayward, based on the novel The Mind of Mr. Reeder by Edgar Wallace. <u>Cast</u>: Will Fyffe, Patricia Roc, Kay Walsh, Lyn Harding, Ronald Shiner, Anthony Holles, Reginald Purdell, Ronald Adams, Maire O`Neill.

Dr O`Dowd, (1940). Warner Brothers; Produced by Samual Sax; Directed by Herbert Mason; Sreenplay by Derek Twist and Austen Melford, based on a story by L.A.G.Strong. <u>Cast</u>: Shaun Glenville, Patricia Roc, Peggy Cummins, Mary Merrall, Liam Gaffney, Walter Hudd, Irene Handl.

Pack up Your Troubles, (1940), Butcher Films; Produced by F.W.Baker; Directed by Oswald Mitchell; Screenplay by Milton Hayward, and Reginald Purdell from a story by Con West. Cast: Reginald Purdell, Wally Patch, Patricia Roc, Wylie Watson, Manning Whiley, Ernest Butcher, G.H.Mulcaster, George.

Three Silent Men, (1940), Butcher Films; Produced by F.W.Baker; Directed by Daniel Birt; Screenplay by Jack Byrd, and Dudley Leslie, based on the book Three Silent Men by E.P.Thorne. Cast: Sebastian Shaw, Derrick de Marney, Patricia Roc, André Morell, Meinhart Maur, John Turnbull.

The Farmer's Wife, (1941). Associated British Picture Corporation; Produced by Walter C Mycroft; Directed by Norman Lee, and Leslie Arliss; Screenplay by Norman Lee, Leslie Arliss and J.E.Hunter, based on a play by Eden Phillpotts. Cast: Basil Sydney, Nora Swinburne, Wilfrid Lawson, Patricia Roc, Michael Wilding, Kenneth Griffith, Betty Warren, Bunty Payne, Viola Lyel, Enid Stamp-Taylor, Edward Rigby, A. Bromley-Davenport, Mark Daly, Jimmy Godden, Davina Craig.

My Wife's Family, (1940). Associated British Picture Corporation; Produced and Directed by Walter Mycroft; Screenplay by Clifford Grey, Norman Lee, from the original play by Harry B. Linton, Fred Duprez and Hal Stephens. Cast: Margaret Scudamore, Patricia Roc, David Tomlinson, John Warwick, Wylie Watson, Chili Bouchier, Joan Greenwood, Peggy Bryan, Leslie Fuller.

Gentleman of Venture (1940). RKO; Produced by W.Victor Hanbury; Directed by Paul L Stein; Screenplay by Nina Jarvis and Paul Merzbach, based on the stage play by Roland Pertwee and John Hastings Turner. Cast: Wilfrid Lawson, Nora Swinburne, Marta Labarr, Ivan Brandt, Reginald Tate, Brian Worth, Edmund Breon, Patricia Roc, Athole Stewart, Thorley Walters, Ruth Maitland, Ian Fleming.

We'll Meet Again, (1943). Columbia; Produced by Ben Henry and George Formby; Directed by Philip Brandon; Screenplay by James Seymour and Howard Thomas. Cast: Vera Lynn, Patricia Roc, Ronald Ward, Donald Gray, Frederick Leister, Betty Jardine, Geraldo.

Let The People Sing, (1942). British National Films; Produced and Directed by John Baxter; Screenplay by John Baxter, Barbara K. Emery and Geoffrey Orme from the novel by J.B.Priestley. Cast: Alastair Sim, Fred Emney, Edward Rigby,

Patricia Roc, Oliver Wakefield, Olive Sloane, Gus McNaughton, Robert Atkins, Richard George, Annie Esmond.

Suspected Person, (1942). Associated British Picture Corporation; Produced and Directed by Lawrence Huntington; Screenplay by Lawrence Huntington. Cast: Clifford Evans, Patricia Roc, David Farrar, Robert Beatty. Anne Firth, William Hartnell, Eric Clavering, Leslie Perrins..

Millions Like Us, (1943). Gainsborough; Produced by Edward (Ted) Black; Directed by Frank Launder and Sidney Gilliat; Screenplay by Frank Launder and Sidney Gilliat. Cast: Patricia Roc, Gordon Jackson, Anne Crawford, Eric Portman, Basil Radford, Naunton Wayne, Moore Marriott, Joy Shelton, Valentine Dunn, Megs Jenkins, Terry Randall, Beatrice Varley, Amy Veness.

2000 Women, (1944). Gainsborough; Produced by Edward Black; Directed by Frank Launder; Screenplay by Frank Launder and Michael Pertwee. Cast: Patricia Roc, Phyllis Calvert, Flora Robson, Renee Houston, Jean Kent, Thora Hird, Muriel Aked, Dulcie Gray, Anne Crawford, Betty Jardine, Hilda Campbell-Russell, Christiana Forbes, Alec Harvey, Jimmy Moore, Bob Arden, Reginald Purdell, Carl Jaffe.

Love Story, (1944). Gainsborough; Produced by Harold Huth; Directed by Leslie Arliss; Screenplay by Leslie Arliss, Doreen Montgomery and Rodney Ackland, from a novel by J.W. Drawbell. Cast: Margaret Lockwood, Stewart Granger, Patricia Roc, Tom Walls, Reginald Purdell, Moira Lister, Dorothy Bramhall, A.E. Matthews, Beatrice Varley, Joan Rees, Vincent Holman.

Madonna of the Seven Moons, (1945). Gainsborough; Produced by R.J. Minney; Directed by Arthur Crabree; Screenplay by Roland Pertwee from the novel by Margery Lawrence. Cast: Phyllis Calvert. Stewart Granger, Patricia Roc, Jean Kent, Peter Glenville, John Stuart, Nancy Price, Reginald Tate, Peter Murray-Hill, Dulcie Gray.

Johnny Frenchman, (1945). Ealing Studios; Produced by Michael Balcon; Directed by Charles Frend; Screenplay by T.E.B. Clarke. Cast: Tom Walls, Françoise Rosay, Patricia Roc, Ralph Michael, Paul Dupuis, Alfie Bass, Beatrice Varley, Frederick Piper, Arthur Hambling, Richard George.

Wicked Lady. (1945). Gainsborough; Produced by R. J. Minney; Directed by Leslie Arliss; Screenplay by Leslie Arliss, Aimee Stuart and Gordon Glennon, from the novel The Life and Death of the Wicked Lady Skelton by Magdalen King-Hall. <u>Cast</u>: Margaret Lockwood, Patricia Roc, James Mason, Griffith Jones, Michael Rennie, Enid Stamp-Taylor, Felix Aylmer, Martita Hunt, David Horne, Jean Kent, Emrys Jones, Amy Dalby, Helen Goss, Ivor Barnard, Muriel Aked.

Canyon Passage, (1946). Universal; Produced by Walter Wagner; Directed by Jacques Tourneur; Screenplay by Ernest Pascal from the novel by Ernest Haycox. <u>Cast</u>: Dana Andrews, Brian Donlevy, Patricia Roc, Susan Hayward, Ward Bond, Andy Devine, Rose Hobart, Lloyd Bridges, Hoagy Carmichael, Fay Holden, Stanley Ridges, Victor Cutler, Onslow Stevens.

When the Bough Breaks, (1947). Gainsborough; Produced Betty Box; Directed by Lawrence Huntington; Screenplay by Muriel Box, Sydney Box and Peter Rogers based on an original story by Herbert Victor and Moie Charles. <u>Cast</u>: Patricia Roc, Rosamund John, Bill Owen, Brenda Bruce, Patrick Holt, Cavan Malone, Leslie Dwyer, Sonia Holm, Torin Thatcher, Catherine Lacey.

So Well Remembered, (1947). RKO/Alliance; Produced by Adrian Scott; Directed by Edward Dmytryk; Screenplay by John Paxton, based on the novel by James Hilton. <u>Cast</u>: John Mills, Trevor Howard, Martha Scott, Patricia Roc, Richard Carlson, Reginald Tate, Beatrice Varley, Frederick Leister, Ivor Barnard, Juliet Mills.

Holiday Camp, (1947). Gainsborough; Produced by Sydney Box; Directed by Ken Annakin; Screenplay by Muriel Box, Sydney Box, and Peter Rogers, from a story by Godfrey Winn. <u>Cast</u>: Jack Warner, Kathleen Harrison, Flora Robson, Dennis Price, Hazel Court, Emrys Jones, Yvonne Owen, Esmond Knight, Jimmy Hanley, Peter Hammond, Esma Cannon, John Blythe, Susan Shaw, Patricia Roc (as herself).

The Brothers, (1947). Triton/Sydney Box; Produced by Sydney Box; Directed by David MacDonald; Screenplay by Muriel Box, Sydney Box and Paul Vincent Carroll, from the novel by L.A. G. Strong. <u>Cast</u>: Patricia Roc. Maxwell Reed, Duncan Macrae, Will Fyffe, Andrew Crawford, Finlay Currie, Megs Jenkins, John Laurie, Morland Graham, James Woodburn, Patrick Boxhill..

Jassy, (1947). Gainsborough. Produced by Sydney Box; Directed by Bernard Knowles; Screenplay by Dorothy Christie, Campbell Christie and Geoffrey Kerr from the novel by Norah Lofts. <u>Cast</u>: Margaret Lockwood, Patricia Roc,

Dennis Price, Basil Sydney, Dermot Walsh, Nora Swinburne, Linden Travers, John Laurie, Esma Cannon, Cathleen Nesbitt, Maurice Denham, Beatrice Varley.

One Night With You, (1948). Two Cities/Rank Produced by Josef Somlo; Directed by Terence Young; Screenplay by Caryl Brahms, and S.J. Simon, from the play Fuga a due voci by Carlo Ludovico Bragaglia. Cast: Patricia Roc, Nino Martini, Hugh Wakefield, Bonar Colleano, Guy Middleton Stanley Holloway, Irene Worth, Charles Goldner.

Retour à la Vie, (1949). (a film in four segments) Film Marceau / Roitfeid-Hoche Production; Produced by Jacques Roitfeld; Directed by Jean Dréville, Georges Lampin, André Cayatte, Henri-Georges Clouzot; Screenplay by Charles Spaak. Segment two, Le 'Retour d'Antoine' d. Jean Dréville – Cast François Perrier, Patricia Roc, Tanis Chandler, Janine Darcey, Max Elloy, Gisèlle Préville.

Black Jack, (1949). Alsa/Jungla Films; Produced and Directed by Julien Duvivier; Screenplay by Julien Duvivier, Charles Spaak, and Michael Pertwee. Cast: George Sanders, Patricia Roc, Agnes Moorehead, Herbert Marshall, Marcel Dalio, Howard Vernon, Dennis Wyndham, José Nieto, José Jaspe.

Man on the Eiffel Tower, (1949). A&T Film Production (Allen/Tone); Produced by Irving Allen; Directed by Burgess Meredith, Charles Laughton, Irving Allen; Screenplay by Harry Brown from the novel A Battle of Nerves by Georges Simenon. Cast: Burgess Meredith, Charles Laughton, Franchot Tone, Robert Hutton, Patricia Roc, Jean Wallace, Wilfred-Hyde White, Belita.

The Perfect Woman, (1949). Two Cities/Rank; Produced by George and Alfred Black; Directed by Bernard Knowles; Screenplay by George Black, Bernard Knowles, and J.B. Boothroyd from a play by Wallace Geoffrey and Basil Mitchell. Cast; Patricia Roc, Nigel Patrick, Stanley Holloway, Miles Malleson, David Hurst, Irene Handl, Pamela Devis, Dora Bryan, Jerry Desmonde.

Son Copain (L`Inconnue de Montréal), (1950). Eclectiques Films, Québec Productions; Produced by Paul L'Anglais; Directed by Jean-Devaire; Screenplay by Charles Exbayat. Cast: Patricia Roc, Paul Dupuis, Alan Mills, René Dary, Albert Dinan, Eliane Dorsay.

Circle of Danger, (1951). Coronado Productions; Produced by David Rose; Directed by Jacques Tourneur; Screenplay by Philip MacDonald from his novel White Heather. Cast: Ray Milland, Patricia Roc, Marius Goring, Hugh Sinclair, Naunton Wayne, Marjorie Fielding, Edward Rigby, Dora Bryan, John Bailey, Colin Gordon, Reginald Beckwith, David Hutcheson, Michael Brennan.

Something Money Can't Buy, (1952). Vic Film Productions; Produced by Joseph Janni; Directed by Pat Jackson; Screenplay by Pat Jackson, and James Landsdale Hodson. Cast: Patricia Roc, Anthony Steel, A.E, Matthews, Moira Lister, David Hutcheson, Michael Trubshawe, Diane Hart, Charles Victor, Henry Edwards, Mary Hinton, Michael Brennan, Roland Curram, Helen Goss.

La Mia vita é tua (My Life is Yours), (1953). Borea Film; Produced and Directed by Giuseppe Masini; Screenplay by Giuseppe Masini Cast: Patricia Roc, Armando Francioli, Alba Arnova, Gemma Bolognesi, Roberto Bruni, Giulio Cali, Mino Doro, Lucien Gallas.

La Vedova X (The Widow), (1955). Venturini/Express. Produced by John G. Nasht and Giorgio Venturini; Directed by Lewis Milestone; Screenplay by Lewis Milestone and Louis Stevens from a novel by Susan York. Cast: Patricia Roc, Massimo Serato, Akim Tamiroff, Anna-Maria Ferrero, Leonardo Botta.

Cartouche, (1954). Venturini/RKO; Produced by John G Nasht; Directed by Steve Sekley; Screenplay by Louis Stevens, Tullio Pinelli. Cast; Patricia Roc, Richard Basehart, Massimo Serato, Akim Tamiroff, Isa Barzizza, Nerio Bernardi, Nino Marchetti, Aldo De Franchi, Vando Tress.

House in the Woods, (1957). Geoffrey Goodhart Productions (As Filmshop); Produced by Geoffrey Goodheart; Directed by Maxwell Munden; Screenplay by Maxwell Munden from a story by Walter C. Crown. Cast: Patricia Roc, Ronald Howard, Michael Gough, Norah Hammond, Bill Shine, Andrea Troubridge, Geoffrey Goodheart.

The Hypnotist, (1957). Merton Park Studios; Prroduced by Alec C. Snowden; Directed by Montgomery Tully; Screenplay by Montgomery Tully from an original play by Falkland L. Cary. Cast: Roland Culver, Patricia Roc, Paul Carpenter, William Hartnell, Kay Callard, Eileen Pollock, Gordon Needham, Mary Jones, Tom Tann, Edgar Driver.

Michael Hodgson

Bluebeard's Ten Honeymoons, (1960). Anglo Allied; Produced by Roy Parkinson; Directed by W. Lee Wilder; Screenplay by Myles Wilder. <u>Cast</u>: George Sanders, Patricia Roc, Corinne Calvet, Jean Kent, Maxine Audley, Harold Berens, George Coulouris, Ian Fleming, Greta Gynt, Ingrid Hafner, Dino Galvini, Paul Whitsun-Jones.

Television Appearances

The Errol Flynn Theatre (1956) Motley Films for ITV; (1 episode) 'Farewell Performance' directed by Lawrence Huntington. <u>Cast</u>: Patricia Roc, Ivan Craig, Conrad Phillips.

White Hunter (1958) Telestar Productions for ITV; (1 episode) 'Pegasus' directed by Don Mullally. <u>Cast</u>: Rhodes Reason, Patricia Roc, Arthur Lawrence, Trevor Reid, Harry Fine.

No Hiding Place (1959) Associated-Rediffusion Television; (1 episode) 'Who is Gustav Varnia' directed by Pat Baker and Bill Morton. <u>Cast</u> : Raymond Francis, Eric Lander, Patricia Roc, Ursula Howells, Charles Gray, Gordon Sterne, Michael Trubshawe.

Skyport (1960) Granada Television; (1 episode) 'Episode No. 1:50' directed by Jean Hamilton. <u>Cast</u>: George Moon, Michael Aldridge, Patricia Roc, Edward Judd, Pauline Stroud, Alan Tilvern, Manning Wilson.

Dixon of Dock Green (1961) BBC Television; (1 episode) 'A Kiss for the Constable directed by Douglas Moodie. <u>Cast</u>: Jack Warner, Peter Byrne, Patricia Roc, Graham Ashley, Hilda Fenemore, Arthur Rigby.

The Saint (1962) Associated Television (ATV); (1 episode) 'The Talented Husband' directed by Michael Truman. <u>Cast</u>: Roger Moore, Derek Farr, Patricia Roc, Shirley Eaton, Donald Churchill, Norman Mitchell.

Bibliography

Barr, Charles, *Ealing Studios* (Los Angeles, University of California Press, 3rd
   edition, 1998)
Barlow, Priscilla, *Wise enough to play the fool: A Biography of Duncan Macrae*
(Edinburgh, John
Donald Publishers, 1995)
Bouchier, Chili, *Shooting Star: The Last of the Silent Film Stars* (London, Atlantis,
   1995)
Box, Muriel, *Odd Woman Out: an autobiography* (London, Leslie Frewin, 1974)
Brown, Geoff, *Launder and Gilliat* (London, British Film Institute, 1977)
Collins, Joan, *Past Imperfect: an autobiography* (London, W.H. Allen, 1984)
Eaton, Shirley, *Golden Girl* (London, B.T. Batsford, 1999)
Granger, Stewart, *Sparks Fly Upward* (London, Granada, 1981)
Halliwell, Leslie, *Halliwell's Film Guide* (London, Harper Collins, various
         editions)
_____*Halliwell's Filmgoer's Companion* (London, Granada, various editions)
Harper, Sue, *Women in British Cinema, Mad Bad and Dangerous to Know* (London,
         Continuum,
2000)
Hird, Thora with Barr, Liz *Not in the Diary* (London, Hodder & Stoughton,
         2000)
Lee, Norman, *Log of a Film Director* (London, Quality Press, 1949)
Lockwood, Margaret, *Lucky Star: the autobiography of Margaret Lockwood*
         (London, Odhams Press, 1953)
Lukins, Jocelyn, *The Fantacy Factory: Lime Grove Studios, London, 1915 – 1991*
         (London, Venta Books, 1996)
Lynn, Vera, *Vocal Refrain: an autobiography*, (London, W.H. Allen, 1975)
Macnab, Geoffrey, *J.Arthur Rank and The British Film Industry* (London,
         Routledge, 1993)
_____*Searching for Stars* (London, Cassell, 2000)
Mason, James, *Before I Forget* (London, Hamish Hamilton, 1981)
McFarlane, Brian, *An Autobiography of British Cinema* (London, Methuen, 1997)
Moreno, Eduardo, *The Films of Susan Hayward* (New Jersey, Citadel Press, 1979)

Morley, Sheridan, *The Other Side of the Moon: the life of David Niven* (London, Weidenfeld & Nicolson, 1985)

Munn, Michael, *Trevor Howard: the man and his films* (London, Robson Books, 1989)

Murphy, Robert, *Realism and Tinsel: Cinema and Society in Britain 1939-1948* (London, Routledge, 1989)

Owen, Bill, *Summer Wine and Vintage Years: a cluttered life* (London: Robson Books, 1994)

Quinlan, David, *Quinlan's Film Directors* (London, B.T. Batsford, 1999)

Pettigrew, Terence, *Trevor Howard* (London, Peter Owen, 2001)

Sanders, George, *Memoirs of a Professional Cad* (New York, G.P. Putnam 1960)

Shiach, Don, *Stewart Granger, The Last of the Swashbucklers* (London, Aurum, 2005)

Spicer, Andrew, *Sydney Box* (Manchester, Manchester University Press, 2006)

Stannage, Robert, *Stars by Day,* (London, The Film Book Club, 1947)

Sweet, Matthew, *Shepperton Babylon; The Lost World of British Cinema* (London, Faber & Faber,2005)

Taraborrelli, J. Randy, *Elizabeth* (London, Sidgwick & Jackson, 2006)

Tims, Hilton, *Once a Wicked Lady: a biography of Margaret Lockwood* (London, Virgin Books, 1989)

_____*Erich Maria Remarque: the last romantic,* (London, Constable, 2003)

Thomson, David, *The New Biographical Dictionary of Film* (London, Little, Brown, 4th edition, 2002)

Warren, Patricia, *British Film Studios: An Illustrated History* (London, B.T. Batsford, 1995)

Newspapers, Magazines, Periodicals etc.

Daily Express, Daily Herald, Daily Mail, Daily Mirror, Daily Sketch, Daily Telegraph, Daily Worker, Evening Standard, Los Angels Times, Manchester Guardian, New York Times, News Chronicle, New Statesman, Scottish Daily Mail, Observer, Sunday Express, Sunday Times.

Catholic News, Kinematograph Weekly, Monthly Film Bulletin, Picturegoer, Picture Post, Picture Show, She Magazine, TV Times, Today's Cinema, Variety.

BFI Dossier 18: Gainsborough Melodrama (British Film Institute, 1983).

Sydney and Muriel Box Diaries (British Film Institute, Special Collection).

The Daily Mail Film Award Annual (Winchester Publications, London, various editions)

Index

Michael Hodgson

About the Author

Michael Hodgson interviewed Patricia Roc, her son, Michael and her sister Bobby many times, as well as surviving co-workers and acquaintances to research this biography. Since the first edition was published in 2010 he has continued to research this remarkable woman, resulting in this much-improved edition.

Brought up in Twickenham, Middlesex and now living in Wiltshire with his wife and two dogs, Michael first became interested in Patricia Roc after gaining a First-class Honours degree in Social History which encompassed the study of the cinema and society in Britain during the 1950s and 1960s, and the social role and cultural influence of film and television in America, Britain and Western Europe.

He is now writing the definitive biography of the J. Arthur Rank star, Anthony Steel, renowned for his whirlwind romance and troubled marriage to the voluptuous Anita Ekberg